D1277707

EMOTIONAL INTELLIGENCE

A Practical Guide to Making Friends with Your Emotions and Raising Your EQ

Positive Psychology Coaching Series

Please be aware that every e-book and "short read" I publish is written truly by me, with thoroughly researched content 100% of the time. Unfortunately, there's a huge number of low quality, cheaply outsourced spam titles on Kindle non-fiction market these days, created by various Internet marketing companies. **I don't tolerate these books. I want to provide you with high quality, so** if you think that one of my books/short reads can be improved anyhow, please contact me at:

contact@mindfulnessforsuccess.com

I will be very happy to hear from you, because that's who I write my books for.

Table of Contents

A VERY Short Preface

Hello, friends! Thanks for grabbing my book. If you've decided to look it up, I guess you already have an idea, even if only a faint one, what **emotional intelligence** (or **emotional quotient (EQ))** is, or might be. Even if you don't, don't worry; you will surely have it all sorted out when you finish reading this book. Not only will it provide you with all the info you need to comprehend what EQ is about, but it will also **give you numerous effective and practical tools you need to dramatically increase your emotional intelligence**, allowing you to gain deep insight into your own and other people's emotions and actions.

I don't like to keep my guests waiting indefinitely in the lobby, so I'm going to invite you in to a great adventure about emotional intelligence in a matter of seconds. Let me just ask you this question:

Do you believe your life would be healthier, happier and even better, if you had more practical strategies to regulate your own emotions?

Most people agree with that. Or, more importantly:

Do you believe you'd be healthier and happier if **everyone who you live with also had the strategies to regulate their emotions?**

Yeah, I know.

Come on in and feel at home! Let's begin!

Introduction
(A Little Bit Longer)

In the last ten years, emotional intelligence has been gaining increasingly more attention all over the world. We heard about it a lot recently. In fact, some people are scared that someday they might find it in their fridge, on a pillow next to them or proudly lying on their doormat one morning... The truth is not too many people actually realize what EQ is really all about, and what causes its popularity to grow constantly. The simplest answer could be found in many scientific studies[1] which clearly show that emotional intelligence is far more important in our lives than the typical intelligence measured by the intelligence quotient (IQ) scale. Scientific research conducted by many American and European universities prove that the "common" intelligence responses account for less than 20% of our life achievements and successes, while the other over 80% depends on emotional intelligence. To put it roughly: either you are emotionally intelligent, or you're doomed to mediocrity, at best.

In 1990, two American psychologists, Peter Salavey and John Mayer, used the term emotional quotient (EQ) for the first time and compared it to "rational intelligence", measured by IQ (although the term "emotional intelligence" was probably seen for the first time in Wayne Payne's 1985 doctoral paper). The sensational news went around the world—we had "two brains". The first one, which we were already familiar with, is responsible for logical thinking and our rational actions. The second one feels and directs our emotions. Psychological research proved numerous times that the intellect alone is not enough to succeed in life.

It all started from following Harvard students' and graduates' careers. It turned out that the people who run big corporations are not the people who used to be the best students, but rather those with quite average IQ levels. Also, two hundred of the largest American companies were researched to find out which characteristics were most common among the best workers. The research revealed that the business leaders excel in these four areas: academic knowledge, IQ level, technical skills and the art of managing their own

---

[1] http://alliance.la.asu.edu/temporary/students/katie/MultipleIntelligenceEmotional.pdf

emotions. This latter category had twice as much impact as all the other areas put together. The last finding of this research was surprising: IQ, knowledge and skills decide whether you fit a certain job, but it is the skill of regulating and maintaining your emotions that allows you to be the best in your area.

When it comes to research on students conducted by *Yale University Center for Emotional Intelligence*, it turns out emotionally intelligent adolescents experience less anxiety, tend to have less depression, and are less likely in middle school and high school to abuse alcohol, cigarettes and drugs. Also, they are less likely to be aggressive and to engage in bullying behaviors. They are more attentive, less hyperactive and they are perceived by their teachers and their peers as being better leaders. They perform better academically, as they have the skills necessary to manage those challenging moments. It's really astounding how useful and powerful emotional intelligence is when it comes to academic performance, social skills and learning.

Does that mean we should only focus on controlling emotions, and neglect or hold down our logical thinking? Further, it was proved the intellect alone, without emotional mastery, doesn't guarantee a success; whereas emotions alone, without the control of reason, can lead us astray. Let's imagine a hypothetical situation: you went out shopping to a supermarket looking for a new washing machine. The choice you have is really abundant and you don't know which model you should choose. If you're a "logical" type of person (guided only by the voice of your mind), you want to buy a model that is the most economical, energy-saving and has a promotional price. When you can't find exactly what you want, you leave the shop and go on searching, wasting lots of time. If you're a "follow-your-heart" type of person (guided by emotional outbursts and feelings), you will probably decide on the first washing machine that catches your eye: a beautiful, colorful, designer model that uses LOTS of energy. In both cases, **your choices would have nothing in common with emotional intelligence.**

Emotionally intelligent people can harmoniously reconcile what their mind and reason tell them with the voice of their emotions and feelings. Thanks to this skill, they're self-confident, self-aware, energetic and creative, as well as capable of handling stress and know how to get along with others. They are optimistically approaching life, don't fear changes and are congruent with themselves. **They are the people of success.**

Think about success—have all prosperous people attained it easily, overnight? Think about J.K Rowling, Stephen King, Steve Jobs, Harland Sanders or anyone else (hundreds of thousands of examples, at least, just taking English speaking countries into consideration), who had to fail A LOT and go through many humiliations in order to finally succeed big time. Let's take J.K Rowling, for example, who is now officially wealthier than the Queen of England—she had two mouths to feed, no job and she was depressed... She was rejected TWELVE TIMES by many different book publishers. Most people would probably lose it at this point, abandon their dreams and take any "ordinary and safe" 9-5 job. Can you imagine how effectively she had to handle her emotions in order to maintain her faith in Harry Potter, in her talent as a writer, and eventually succeed? Stephen King was addicted to alcohol and he lived with his wife in an indigent trailer. Yet, he was emotionally intelligent and he won over himself. Jobs was kicked out of his own company, Apple, started another two companies, which also had a great impact on today's world, and then came back to Apple as a winner. I know you might think, "You are talking about big shots, intelligent people. It's like winning the lottery anyway." HOWEVER, if you're dreaming about a satisfying career and any success at all, no matter if you want to be a famous musician, manager, lawyer, headhunter, CEO, writer or President of the United States, then the truth is you will fail a lot. I'm not being pessimistic here—it's just like you will fall a lot when you're learning how to ride a bike, and you will swallow gallons of water when you're learning how to swim for the first time. It's normal and it's a part of the process, but either you are emotionally intelligent enough to handle your negative emotions on the way, or you will quit before you even get started.

After all, this great discovery about "two brains" is just the reminder of facts already known to the physiology of the nervous system. Emotional intelligence is the ability to coordinate features of the cerebral cortex, evolutionarily the youngest part of the brain and the section that determines the level of IQ, with the most primitive emotional brain, which evolved much earlier than the "thinking brain". The emotional brain allowed our ancestors to survive in extreme conditions, when decisions of "fight or flight" were crucial for the preservation of life. In present times, where we don't have to climb trees to escape saber-toothed, armored badgers (okay, guilty—I have no idea if such a creature ever existed, but you know what I mean...), and our survival depends rather on the number of zeros in our bank account, we sent our emotional brain to the bullpen. Now, we are trying to restore its esteem and the recognition of its necessity.

What makes emotional intelligence have such a big impact on our lives? We, human beings, make most of our decisions and take most action based on our feelings and emotions. If we know how to control and navigate them, we thus gain the ability to better manage both our personal and professional lives.

How to Use This Book

This book is stuffed with lots of effective exercises, helpful info and practical ideas. Every chapter covers different areas of emotional intelligence and shows you, step by step, what exactly you can do to develop your EQ and become the better version of yourself.

If you want to really profit from reading it, you need to **take action** and **stick to practicing** all these things I write about. You need regularity and persistence, because what's the good in reading all these books, watching videos and attending seminars, when you do not act on them? It's more or less just a waste of your time. Seriously, you could be better off and healthier to spend that time sleeping.

Having said that, some of these ideas and exercises will be simple and easy, but they're all scientifically and personally (by myself, my co-workers, friends and clients) proven to be very effective. You can either try each of them after you're done reading each chapter, or read the whole book and then come back to practice those you think might be the most helpful for you. Many of these exercises will tell you to use visualization techniques. If you feel you're not too good with visualizing things or your imagination could be improved, begin with taking a look into Bonus Chapter: Visualizations 101.

Before we begin—remember—emotional intelligence is a skill, and can be learned through constant practice and training, just like riding a bike or swimming! I've changed myself, my friends have seen results, and so can you.

Are you ready?

Let's start!

Chapter 1: When You Lack Social Intelligence...

As opposed to the popular image, emotionally intelligent people are **not** the ones who react impulsively and spontaneously, or who act lively and fiery in all types of social environments.

Kate and Eve, although sensitive, are not emotionally intelligent.

Kate is a young head of the department in one of the large companies. At the very first meeting of the team she announced, "The atmosphere at work is the most important thing for me; I always say what I think and I do not tolerate gossiping." She often spoke about her emotions at work. When she felt nervous, she would shout and slam the doors. When the team was successful, she would jump up and down with joy and laugh out loud. Employees competed in guessing her moods. If it was good, they could arrange almost everything with her. Unfortunately, Kate often changed her own decisions. Moreover, she carelessly attributed the success of others to herself, and often punished the employees for her own mistakes.

Eve, a single mom, says that love needs to be well tended. She and her daughter Caroline talk to each other a lot, know each other's secrets and seem to have a strong bond. One day, a "bomb" explodes—Eve finds out her daughter has been arrested for shoplifting, while under the influence of drugs. Even though Caroline assures her that it was her first time and it won't happen again, Eve doesn't know how to forgive her and how to forget about it. She feels betrayed and guilty as a parent. She suffers and leaves her high school-aged daughter home alone for a few weeks, without any further information and with her phone turned off. She stays at her old friend's place, cries every night and goes through her "failure" again and again. She can't trust her daughter for another couple of years.

Let's now imagine Kate and Eve went through EQ coaching, knowing how to deal with their emotions and respecting other people's feelings.

Kate comes to the realization that the atmosphere at work depends both on her and the entire team. She listens to what her employees have to say, she cares about their opinions, and she controls her emotions. Every time she has a bad day and makes a mistake, she has the courage to apologize for her behavior. She chooses to learn from employees that are better than her in certain areas, rather than bringing them down. She knows that as the head of the department, she has to be an authority. She does not get overly familiar with anyone and doesn't expose too much of her personal life and feelings. She never criticizes people themselves, but gives constructive criticism of their behavior. She knows how to praise her coworkers to motivate them, and does it often. She often repeats that successful companies are the merit of the whole team and promotes her workers for all their great projects.

When Eve finds out what her daughter did, she's in a big shock. She asks her daughter to talk with her honestly, but only when the first excitement has subsided and they can calmly talk about what happened. Although Eve is really angry and feels a huge resentment towards Caroline, she tries not to offend or harass her. She mainly tells Caroline about her emotions: "I'm sorry. I felt hurt. I didn't deserve such horrible news and I really thought we were fair and honest with each other," and so on. At the end, she says she really loves Caroline and cares about her future. Her daughter feels guilty and admires her mom's calm, collected and mature behavior. They both try to understand why Caroline did what she did, and where the dishonesty in their relationship came from. They still want to be close to each other as single mother and daughter, but they know their relationship has to change. They both decide to seek a professional family therapist, until everything clears between them.

Putting emotions first is **not** synonymous with the ability to manage them at work and in private life. One can be very emphatic, but at the same time lack the skills that translate to being a good boss or a partner. Emotional intelligence **doesn't** equal getting rid of emotional control, being nice or submissive. Most psychologists claim the level of EQ is not genetically shaped. **Emotional intelligence can be learned and developed throughout life.**

Emotionally intelligent people are open to new experiences, can show feelings adequate to the situation, either good or bad, and find it easy to socialize with other people and establish new contacts. They handle stress well, say "no" easily, realistically assess the achievements of themselves or others, and are not afraid of constructive criticism and taking calculated risks. Unfortunately, this perfect model of an emotionally intelligent person is extremely rare in our modern times.

Sadly, nowadays the amount of emotional problems in the world is increasing at an alarming rate. We are getting richer, but less and less happy. Depression, suicide, relationship breakdowns, loneliness by choice, fear of closeness, addictions—these are clear evidence that we are getting increasingly worse when it comes to dealing with our emotions.

The cult of information and rational thinking in modern society often leads to these and many other pathologies in our experience of life. People put information on a pedestal, giving it highest priority, and are a little bit obsessed with consistently getting new information/knowledge, even if that information or knowledge is totally useless. The biggest mistake in this world is the fact that everyone has a brain, but no one is given a manual along with it. I only know a few people who are able to consciously control their thoughts, redirect their focus and wisely release or regulate their feelings. This should be a brick of fundamental elementary education both in schools and in homes! Of course, medical companies already have their answer for this problem—do you feel stressed? Here, take the pills, grab a handful, swallow them boldly, go, go, go! What are you waiting for?!? Shove them into your mouth, and help yourself with a little water. Don't even think about the side-effects, **or about changing yourself**.

We forget that besides logic and verbal reasoning, we also have the ability to explore and experience the world in a nonverbal way. I will show you how freeing yourself from the domination of left-sided brain thinking can contribute to your inner transformation—the emotional revolution that will help you redefine who you are and what you really want from life.

It's easy to notice the left hemisphere of the brain dominates everyday actions of most people, as it's responsible for language, rational reasoning, logic and facts. Nowadays, you are flooded with information wherever you look—TV news, newspapers, magazines, Internet on almost every single device, Google, Facebook, YouTube—social pressure of continuous acquisition of knowledge, the cult of "rational thinking". Take a look around and notice how many people mindlessly stuff their heads with useless knowledge and worthless data, not because they need them or want to learn something, but because *"you should expand your knowledge"* and *"you should know what's going on in the world."*

Well, if you're constantly watching TV news, which almost always shows manipulated and biased views of the world, designed to manipulate the masses, then you surely won't see reality for what it really is.

"The world of America is as big as their newspaper."

Albert Einstein

"Logic: The art of thinking and reasoning in strict accordance with the limitations and incapacities of the human misunderstanding."

Ambrose Bierce

"Imagination is more important than knowledge. For knowledge is limited to all we know and understand, while imagination embraces the entire world, and all there ever will be to know and understand."

Albert Einstein

The rational mind, or so called "reason", has become the most important tool of modern man. While rational thinking is a great achievement of human evolution indeed, it is totally useless on its own, as a stand-alone tool. Take a look back and think how many times you tried to solve a problem or make a correct decision only with rational thinking. How many times did it turn out to be impossible or totally inaccurate?

This everlasting flood of verbal stimuli keeps our left hemisphere working at maximum capacity, drowning out the world of emotions, creativity, imagination and intuition—all the aspects of our existence for which the right hemisphere of the brain is responsible. We are constantly being called on all sides to push our emotions away. *"Think rationally!"* *"Emotions have too big an impact on you!"* *"Do not act under the influence of your emotions!"*

Robert Wolcott Sperry, a famous American neuropsychologist and 1981 Nobel Prize winner, once said:

"The main theme to emerge is that there appear to be two modes of thinking, verbal and nonverbal, represented rather separately in left and right hemispheres, respectively, and that our educational system, as well as science in general, tends to neglect the nonverbal form of intellect. What it comes down to is that modern society discriminates against the right hemisphere."

This social narrative results in one very pathological mechanism—lack of acceptance of our emotions. Most people think emotions are bad, that one shouldn't feel them, nor give in to them at all.

What is the result of this type of thinking? Destructive emotions overlap and become even stronger. A boy who is sad after he broke up with his girlfriend might additionally start feeling angry because, *"I shouldn't be so weak!"* Then, not only does he have to deal with his sadness, but also with anger, as well as the new feeling that emerged when sadness

14

and anger combined into one. It is very difficult to work with such an emotional state. Before the sadness gets accepted, he will have to have the ability to observe and deal these emotions. Acceptance, awareness and insight into certain emotions are the key to getting rid of them.

Suppression of the emotions felt makes you lose touch with yourself. It makes you stop accepting yourself. It makes you tell yourself, *"I have to feel great at all times."* The denial of emotion distances us from the voice of intuition, and leads to continuous and often pointless verbal thoughts.

It should be pointed out that rational thinking is a skill evolution created way after emotional mechanisms, not before them. Emotions are just as important, if not more important, as rational thought and are part of who we are.

So, let's look at the famous, *"Never act on your emotions,"* from a different angle.

The greatest achievements are possible only if you work under the influence of passion, inspiration, motivation, inner joy and creativity! These are the emotions that strongly stimulate us to take action and achieve our goals. Unfortunately, when people displace their negative emotions, in turn they deny their emotionality as a whole, thus losing access to the constructive emotions.

When you open yourself to the right hemisphere's experiences and understanding of the world, you discover a whole new reality. You deal with your own emotional states much better, and you understand others, yourself and your actions. It's easier for you to choose the right path in life. You start listening to your intuition, which always suggests to you the best solutions. You start feeling real, positive emotions, such as pure joy, full happiness or deep gratitude increasingly often. That's the road that will lead you to the discovery of your true potential. You will flourish like a beautiful flower, or turn from a caterpillar into a colorful butterfly.

That being said, it's a process you need to stick to. The release of certain emotions, gaining control over some other feelings and getting in tune with your own intuition require regular work and appropriate tools. Effects of the work and process are astonishing and have the potential to initiate a deep, inner transformation in you.

What are the simplest things you could do at the very beginning?

The first one I will give you is very simple—SLOW DOWN a little bit (if possible... but unless you are a single mother of four, it is almost always possible).

If you work twelve hours a day, six days a week, and during weekends, instead of relaxing and spending time with friends and family, then waste your off-hours watching too much news on TV or gossiping, you are constantly expressing negative and toxic emotions. You are not too likely to heal your relationships with other people and yourself this way.

Even the best coach or therapist can't predict all of your emotional reactions and give you advice how to act in every possible life situation. Instead of reading newspapers and watching TV that show you the same, subjective and stuffed with negative messages model of reality, **start discovering the world on your own.** Start searching for alternative sources of information.

Take informational detox for some time. Turn off the TV (or ideally, throw it out the window, it's usually useless), and limit your time online. You could even take some time off from books (not too much, though!). Commit your free time to work on yourself, in meditation and reflection on the issues important to you. Start experiencing more, trying new things. Do not judge these experiences verbally. Instead, check out how you feel in new situations.

We also often forget that all our emotions begin in the body. Let's assume that you're angry. You feel tension in the muscles, feel increased heart rate and you also breathe faster—that's the evolutionarily oldest part of the brain awakening and preparing the body for fight or flight.

That's why it's a very good idea to start the training by working with your body—you need to realize what exactly happens with you when you are experiencing strong emotions, both positive and negative. This kind of training takes time, but it's necessary. Until you learn how to accurately read, name and express emotions in a manner that is harmless both for you and others, you won't be able to really understand yourself and other people.

Those were just a few advice points that will give you some basic ideas and help you take the first step towards the "liberation" of your right hemisphere. To act effectively, you want both hemispheres to work together for you.

Note: The "right and left hemisphere thinking" theory has been debunked and classified as a popular-psychology myth, or oversimplification, by many academic neuropsychologists, as in reality we usually use both hemispheres at the same level of intensity to solve the majority of our problems, whether logical or creative. For the sake of the chapter above, I used the right and left side thinking as a metaphor of the emotional/creative/intuitive/inquisitive mind vs. rational/logical mind, where each of them can be reinforced and put to work more effectively. In this book, I will obviously focus on developing and strengthening the emotional/inquisitive mind.

Chapter 2: What Does EQ Consist of?

Emotional intelligence (EQ)—a term popularized by Daniel Goleman—is, in the simplest words, an ability to recognize your and other people's emotions.

Should we look closer into that definition, we would learn not only does EQ consist of emotional competencies, but also social. The former comes down to:

- **Self-awareness** – knowledge about your emotional states.
- **Adequate self-esteem** – awareness of your limits, capabilities and possibilities. It's also experiencing yourself, regardless of other people's judgements.
- **Self-regulation/self-control** – control over your emotions: not succumbing to impulses, or the conscious response to the outside world.

Whereas, talking about social competencies, we can talk about:

- **Empathy** – **understanding** (not necessarily feeling) other people's emotional states in certain situations; it's also an ability to feel and understand social relations.
- **Assertiveness** – having and expressing your own opinion and beliefs, even against the majority.
- **Persuasion** – an ability to trigger certain behaviors and actions in other people.
- **Leadership** – an ability to generate ideas and engage others in these ideas.
- **Cooperation** – an ability to effectively collaborate with others, work as a team, the ability to work towards common goals.

Three Pillars of Emotional Intelligence

Mastery in this area will give you great emotional wisdom—you will get to know yourself from a side that you didn't have any idea ever existed. This is the key both to building relationships with other people, and guiding them towards achieving great goals.

Emotions are an integral part of our lives; without them, we are unable to function in society, if at all. Even if you're not aware of it and you feel "neutral", most of the time you are in some kind of emotional state. There's a possibility that, in this very moment, you feel emotions of curiosity about what are you going to read next. Or you're irritated because your annoying neighbor is mowing the lawn for the fifth time this week and his dog is accompanying him, barking all the time.

You've already read about the popular distinction between the logical mind and the emotional mind earlier in this book. While, in fact, there's no such thing as clear, rational thinking. It was proven a long time ago, in serious injury cases where areas of the brain responsible for emotions were damaged, that a man without emotion is **not able to cope with life.** With their emotions disabled, human beings **can't even make the simplest decisions**, such as selecting what to eat for breakfast or which shoes to wear.

Unfortunately, school has not taught us how to recognize and control our emotions. That's why the majority of people on this planet are on extreme opposites. **Their emotions are so strong that their whole life is subordinated to what they feel.** Not only does this inability to cope with suffering, sulks, anger and other unpleasant feelings hold them back from achieving success in life, it also takes all the fun out of ordinary day-to-day existence.

That's why it's worth it to invest your time and energy in emotional intelligence training. One decade ago, I had no idea how to cope with the bad emotions in my life. Thanks to constant work, the way I will show you further in this book, I finally changed the roles. Now, I'm in control of my emotions, not the other way around.

There's one thing you have to remember—you can regulate your emotions. Once again, it is a skill, like any other. Calming down the unpleasant feelings when necessary, reinforcing the positive ones, whenever you want. In every single moment of your life, you can feel exactly as you want to feel. It will guide you directly to the conscious life in which creating lasting relationships and making new challenges will be accompanied by excitement and enjoyment rather than fear and stress.

Of course, all these things relate to both negative and positive emotions. In addition to the ability to control those nasty emotions, you also want to learn how to produce powerful, rich emotional states, such as motivation, enjoyment and self-confidence. Here are the three pillars you need to achieve to increase your emotional intelligence:

I. Be Aware of the Emotions You Feel

This is the absolute foundation for any work with emotions. Most people do not even realize the emotions that arise in their body. Some, on the other hand, are aware of the feelings, but this realization appears a long time after the occurrence of a given emotion. The situation you ideally want to have is where the time between the emergence of each emotion and thought ("Oh! I feel angry right now! Yes, it is anger!") will be as short as possible. You can't change who you are until you are aware of something that needs to be changed. Emotional intelligence is mainly about awareness; the beauty of EQ is when you bring something to your awareness and you practice with different responses, you can really change your brain. You've probably already reflected on numerous fields where the ability to call and identify emotional states has a BIG impact in life. It's nothing strange, as emotions have immense power over us from the day we're born.

The sooner you realize that a certain feeling is present in you right now, the more control over it you can gain.

The very fact of the emerging consciousness about each emotion allows you to access a "higher level", dissociating from the emotion to some extent. According to the spiritual master Osho, awareness of emotions begins the process of their dissolution. Practice this awareness by exactly observing your body and being aware of every emotion that arises inside. More about this later in this book.

II. Know Your Emotions

This is the most important of the three pillars of emotional intelligence.
Knowing your emotions consists of obtaining answers to the four questions below.

1. Where did they come from? What's going on in your head in the moment before the emotion appears? What thought triggers this feeling?

Any time you are about to recognize emotions, consider what caused their formation. What belief or thought sounded in your head for a moment before they appeared? If you do not remember any thought, just ask yourself, "Why do I feel like this?" Once you find the reason, you will have found **very important information**: knowledge about what type of thinking fires such emotional states inside of your body.

2. Where and when did they start? Every emotion has its place in your body.

Interestingly, each person feels the same emotions in different ways. When conducting individual coaching or training, I often had the opportunity to see how one person felt stress as a sand-like substance in their throat, and another as severe as corrosive acid in their thighs and calves.

When an emotion appears, close your eyes and find where exactly in your body it is located and where the emotion starts. Discover how the emotion comes to life. Is it a sudden explosion or a slow birth?

3. What is the course and the intensity of these emotions?

With your eyes still closed, examine how a given emotion is developing in your body. Which direction is it going? How does it do so? To make it easier, you can try to imagine its form, shape, color, exact size, temperature, etc. Thanks to this exercise, you will be able to better examine the structure of your emotions and notice how they live and work in your body. Also, think whether it is a strong emotion, or a rather weak one.

4. How and where do they end? How long do they last?

Think of a time when the given emotion disappears. What's the reason it starts evaporating? Has enough time passed, or is it the result of any special thought? How does the emotion end—is it going back to its initial form, or maybe disappearing all at once? How long did this emotion last—five minutes or maybe a few hours?

As soon as you collect all the answers to the questions above, you will have gathered a priceless collection of information on that specific emotion you feel. It will make you take a great step forward—you probably never knew this much about one specific emotion, until now. Thanks to this information, you gain the ability to control it, because you know where it comes from, how it grows and when it takes over.

When I first started using this approach, I got really surprised how accurate an insight I could have into my emotions. I was never aware, for example, that a feeling of joy in my body begins in the middle of the abdomen and then spreads upwards.

Ask yourself these questions in regard to any emotions you feel. **After some time, consciously figuring it out and actively thinking about it is no longer needed.** You will just naturally feel every single emotion appearing in your body, and immediately you will know everything about it. This is what I call emotional intelligence, which becomes a source of many positive changes in your emotional and physical world.

III. Control Your Emotions

Mastering the second point will give you basic control of your emotions. The third point is to bring the control to the next, more advanced level.

Here, however, a more tenacious training is required—regular practice of certain exercises, which after some time will bring results in the form of full control of your emotions. Again, if you just go through this book without taking any action, it will turn to another dust-gathering knickknack on your bookshelf, or just another file on your Kindle or tablet. **If you want to change yourself, you have to PRACTICE. No one's going to change yourself for you!**

The best way to control your emotions is to effectively control your thoughts. In this book, you will read about quite a few effective exercises that will help you stay in charge and acquire better understanding of yourself—your emotions, actions and beliefs. You will also become a better communicator.

In addition, there are many tools to change emotions in the mighty arsenal of neuro-linguistic programming (NLP). Among others, there's a change of submodalities, about which you will also read later in this book.

Apply these tools regularly, and you will master your emotions entirely. It takes work, but the results can be amazing.

That's actually all you need to know about the basics of emotional intelligence. Of course, this topic is much deeper and includes many different areas, like the issues causing strong emotional states in yourself and in others, the achievement of deep empathy, or the ability to create messages containing a whole array of emotions.

In the beginning, focus on the first two foundations of emotional intelligence. Their mastery will give you extraordinary results in practically every possible area of your life. When you play with them a little bit, you can go on and start working on the third pillar to bring your skills to the next level, about which you are going to read now.

Let's start!

Chapter 3: Observing and Expressing Your Emotions

Lack of free emotional expression is exactly what forces people to wear masks, while hiding all the things they are afraid of showing to the outside world. Repressed emotions have a habit of coming back with twice the intensity, and so we often end up with the helpless, "*I don't know how to deal with my emotions!*"

Smothering and suppression of the emotions causes many, often very subtle, psychological biases and damage, which manifest themselves in our everyday life. Fortunately, there is an alternative where the emotions are just like clouds in the spring sky. They come and go, fully accepted.

Emotional denial is a consequence of the social belief that emotions are bad. That we shouldn't feel negative emotions. That emotions have to be fully controlled at all times and suppressed.

What's the outcome? Some people deny their emotions so intensely, they have no idea at all what and how they're feeling in a given moment. They barely feel anything and are torn between thinking about the future and the past so much, they don't even bother asking themselves, "What emotions are present in me at this very moment?"

By suppressing emotion, we accumulate lots of excess energy inside our nervous systems, which is **very harmful** for our health, both mentally and physically.

A person who has a minimal awareness of their own emotional states can sometimes have a glimpse of "*I'm so angry!*" or "*I'm so terribly nervous before tomorrow's exam!*" but that is nothing more than a brief one-second look through the keyhole into the chamber in which a wealth of knowledge and precious information about the person is being kept.

Such a glimpse is not enough. We need awareness. Insight. Recognition. This will allow us to free all these emerging emotions, while fully accepting their temporary presence.

Please remember the last time when you felt joy. How did it feel? The majority of people will just say, *"Pleasant,"* and that will be the end of their retrospection. Such a shallow insight won't allow them to understand their emotions and fully recall this feeling.

Instead, it's really good to focus on each emotion for a moment. Think about it, why did you feel it? When did you start to feel joy? Where in your body is this feeling located? Analyze all these details very carefully.

Recently, I came across an interesting lecture by Eckhart Tolle, where he talks about observing our emotions. He says the expression of destructive emotions is not enough. Screaming with rage or crying like a baby gives a vent to the energy in you, but does not cure the root of the problem (of course, it is worth it to give this energy release, but it can be done in more constructive ways, such as going for a run). After you rest, the emotion may appear again. The energy, fed with destructive thinking, takes the form of destructive emotions.

Therefore, Eckhart suggests something more, "Express your emotions while watching this process." The second part of this quote is the key here, because expressing emotions alone may not give you the desired effect, as unobserved emotions will keep coming back. Observation gives you the awareness of how your thoughts generate emotions you then feel in your body.

Additionally, the process of observation results in so called "depersonalization", which means that you will stop identifying yourself with the emotions. You cease to see them as an integral part of your existence, as a part of you, and begin to see them as clouds passing in the sky, separate from your own Self.

That's the exact difference between "I am angry!" and "I am experiencing anger."

I noticed the observation of my own emotions during their expression gives an incredible awareness of the processes, which previously I had no idea even existed.

You notice more, understand more, and hence accept more.

Simply close your eyes for a moment and direct all your attention inwards.

Concentrate on the sensations that arise at the center of your being.

Observe in the silence.

Allow your emotions to be, without losing your precious energy to sweep it under the rug. Even if they are not pleasant, accept their presence anyway. As a result, their visit in your body will be much shorter and less noticeable. **Just like every cloud, after a while they will quietly drift away.**

Remember to watch your emotions without judgment. Put aside your beliefs about the feelings of anger, jealousy, stress or fear. Instead, tell yourself you want to know the true nature of these emotional states. This is pure observation, which gives you the most valuable insight, not contaminated with your mental filters.

Note everything you have observed. The conclusions may turn out to be very important discoveries for you.

Chapter 4: How to Release Destructive Emotions and Empower the Positive Ones

"I hate being sad!" said a frustrated and angry entrepreneur, before one of the seminars I was attending begun. Sadness plus anger results in an interesting, but vicious emotional mix. It's upsetting, but also a little bit funny, how often we feel blocked by the obstacles WE alone create for ourselves.

Let's begin with a very important question: Do you require emotional perfection from yourself? Do you always expect yourself to feel good and sustain a positive attitude towards your life?

If the answer was "yes," you are shooting yourself in the foot. You are becoming an obstacle for yourself.

Why?

Because every time the less pleasant emotions come—anger, frustration, sadness, disappointment—you will feel even worse, as you will say to yourself, "I should feel good and happy all the time, no matter what!"

It is a common ailment of the people paying too much attention to self-development (or self-dev. newbies), *"Being sad is for wimps!"* That's so brilliant. Are you angry? Then you should be angry at yourself because you just got angry. It makes perfect sense, if you ask me. Then, feel resentment for the anger you just felt because you felt the anger. Not too smart, is it? Yet, an amazingly huge number of people still do it. I never conducted any scientific research on that on my own, but I estimate it's a vast majority of the people inhabiting this humble blue planet. They basically overlay destructive emotions with even more unnecessary negative emotions, thereby preparing themselves a cocktail of very unpleasant feelings, which is very hard to swallow and also quite stinky, if you ask me. **They literally make a problem out of problem, at their own request.**

The vicious cocktail of "sadness + anger + stings of remorse" is a hard nut to crack. How do you then find a way out from this detrimental neurochemical puddle which drowns your brain and makes clear and sane thinking close to impossible?

Take away this: **Every single negative emotion is an arrow sign pointing towards a problem which needs your attention!** Whenever you judge your emotions (*"I shouldn't be feeling this way."*), you can't see the problem and you're stuck in this negative state... Well, you are actually making it even harder and worse. When you overlay your bad emotions with even more negative feelings, you just cover the essence of your challenge with a thick stinky blanket and lose your access to it.

Whenever you feel bad, accept it and, for your own sake, don't throw more wood onto the fire! However banal it might sound, most people never act this way, making their lives miserable every single day with the stubbornness of one hundred donkeys. Acceptance will only help give you clear insight. **What is insight?** Insight takes place when you look inside of yourself and spend some time with your emotional state, all alone, face to face. Only when you learn how to observe the primary emotion (the one that appeared first as a result of a certain situation or a thought), can you open the doors to understanding this emotion. **Only then can you truly express it and release it.**

Focus on how you feel different negative emotions. It could be frustration, anger or disappointment. **Submerge into these emotions like a professional scuba diver.** Ask yourself: what's this emotion for? Where did it come from? What does it want to tell me? What can I do to make it go away? Then, and only then, will you discover a whole new world, which you never had any idea existed, so you couldn't access it or even get close.

The very foundation of emotional intelligence is emotional awareness, meaning the ability to identify your emotions and express them. Open and clear expression of your emotions, in front of yourself as well, is the best way to release them. When you smother your emotions or pretend they are not there, you just accumulate them and thus torture yourself, allowing them to haunt you endlessly. Remember: telling yourself lies isn't a smart strategy, nor a long-term one.

Enough talking! Let's now focus on something practical. Here's the exercise that will help you understand and release unpleasant emotions, but also help you experience the positive ones more deeply and fully.

<u>Exercise I</u>

What are the profits of this exercise?

- Greater awareness of the emotions felt
- The ability to name, express and release negative emotions
- The ability to deepen positive emotional states.

Take a look at the scheme below:

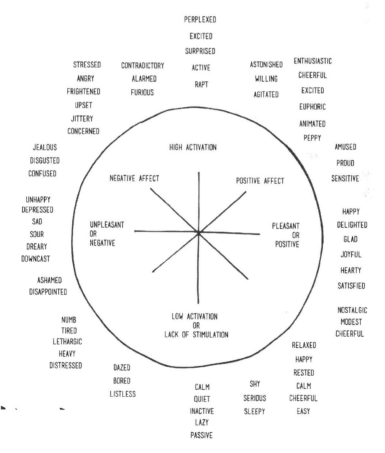

1. Take some time to get familiar with all these emotions, then pick two or three you are feeling now or felt earlier today. I also encourage you to work with positive emotions. This exercise will help you feel them more in depth.

2. Sit comfortably, close your eyes and bring this feeling back. Focus all your attention on the sensations that appear in your body. Allow yourself to remain in this state for a moment and observe it carefully.

3. Describe this feeling. The best way to do this is to say it aloud. You can do it in many different ways, for example:

- Using a metaphor, e.g. *"The fear I feel is like a ..."*;

- Telling a simple story about this feeling;

- Describing mental and physical sensations connected with that state of mind.

4. Examine how you feel after describing this emotion. Did the deeper understanding change the way you feel the emotion? If the emotion was not pleasant, has the level of discomfort diminished? If the emotion was good, have you succeeded in feeling it more fully?

You can take this exercise with you everywhere you go. Every single time you notice a strong emotional state inside of yourself, stop for a moment and name it. A few times a day ask yourself, **"How do I feel right now?"**

Every time the situation allows you to do so, dive into that emotion and present it to yourself in a few sentences. Fully focus all your attention on the emotion you feel and describe it as specifically as you possibly can.

This exercise will give you significantly deeper understanding of the emotional states that accompany you every day. **The deeper the understanding, the bigger the**

acceptance. If you stick to it, once and for all, you will be finished with serving yourself toxic cocktails and poisonous potions that oftentimes make your life so miserable.

By setting yourself free from bad emotional habits, you will make more space in your life for good emotions. Observe how they germinate and slowly grow every day in a variety of situations—this classic golden nugget can't be said enough: energy goes where the attention flows. Remember, what you feed your attention with will develop and strengthen.

Let me now show you more exercises to help you become more aware of your emotions and your goals. It's important that you do them before reading the next chapters.

Exercise II

Reflect on yesterday. Take a piece of paper and write down which emotions you felt during each hour. Try also writing down approximately how long every emotion lasted.

If it's possible, try to also do it with a few previous days. This will allow you to get more data to your average score and, in turn, see more. Of course, the farther the date, the more difficult it will be to remember which emotional states you experienced, but you don't have to be super-precise here. It's not a Swiss watch factory. You can just come up with your estimation. After you're done writing everything down, see what's the ratio of positive vs. negative emotional states you had experienced during these days.

Exercise III

Think how would you like that ratio to be after you finish reading this book—how much would you like the ratio of time spent feeling positive emotions to increase and how much would you like the ratio of time spent on negative emotions to decrease? Come up with realistic values you feel you could achieve. Remember, no one feels good and happy 100% of the time (even psychopaths) and no one can control their emotions in e-v-e-r-y possible situation, every single time. On the other hand, **you can hugely increase the amount of time you feel good emotions each day.**

Starting today, you should continue doing this exercise on a daily basis for another couple of weeks. It will allow you to observe and stay up-to-date with your progress in learning emotional intelligence.

Exercise IV

Start a journal, in which you will be writing down all the emotions you have felt every single day.

You should look on it as an interesting journey and adventure that will allow you to understand yourself, your emotions, and your strong and weak points. The realization of what emotions affected you every single day is not enough, though. You want to get to the point where you realize you feel certain emotions at the very second they come to you and start emerging in your body. You will get to that and keeping a journal will help you a lot.

Divide the sheet of paper into two columns: narrow and wide. In the first (narrow) column, write down all the emotions that appeared during the previous day at work (or home, if there's where you work). Start from the first moments in the office/factory/department, wherever it is you are working, the emotions that accompanied you during your morning tea or coffee, meetings with co-workers, employees or employers, patients, your colleagues, partners, bosses, CEOs, etc. Then, proceed to the emotions which appeared during the second part of the day, and so on, until those you feel when you're leaving your place of work.

In the second (wide) column, write down the context in which these emotions appeared. Did fear show up only when you realized that you were going to be late for the business meeting? Was joy connected with lunch break, or maybe with a new challenge that was put in front of you?

Exercise V

Stable self-esteem is one of the qualities of emotional intelligence. The purpose of this exercise is to look at the factors affecting your confidence throughout the day.

Before you start this exercise, draw or print a few car speedometers.

Think about important people in your life and work.

Mark on the printed speedometers which level your self-confidence is at when interacting with each of these people. Maybe you feel confident when you're talking to your co-worker from another department, but your bravery ends when you come across your rival from the same office or your mean manager? You can also mark the level of self-confidence you feel during different events from your professional life. How would you describe your self-confidence when you got promoted, and how was it when you received negative feedback from your supervisor?

Additional questions to this exercise:

- Is your level of self-confidence stable, or maybe dependent on external factors?

- Around which people do you feel the most confident, and around which do you feel bad and worthless?

- How are you affected by your successes and failures?

- When would the feeling of low self-esteem motivate you, and when would it discourage you?

- Now the opposite: when has your high self-esteem made you lazy, and when did it drive you to make your actions more effective and solid?

Supplemental questions to all four above exercises:

- Which emotions dominate your days at work?

- What causes them? Certain people, unexpected situations, memories? Something else?

- If you were to perceive all the negative emotions as signals about your unmet needs, which needs would you write down?

- What can you do with the emotions you feel? How can you change them by changing their triggers? For example, if you often feel irritated because you have under-slept, maybe you should increase your wellness by cutting off Internet surfing and going to bed earlier.

- You should also use another page of your journal to do the same exercise, but now focusing on the emotions that come to you when you're spending your time at home, with family or with friends (your free time, in general).

Starting today, begin paying attention to all these emotions, both positive and negative, that come to you thorough the day. The previous chapter, "Three Pillars of Emotional Intelligence," will help you with that.

These exercises won't be the easiest in the beginning, as initially you will probably forget to pay attention to your emotions all the time. However, it gets simpler with each day of doing that. You can begin with setting an alarm clock on your phone to remind you to analyze your emotions in that moment.

Chapter 5: Submodalities

Every thought you create in your mind has certain parameters. These are the "submodalities", i.e. the characteristics of images, sounds and feelings of the basic mental processes. Changing submodalities has many uses; it can be applied to treat phobias, change beliefs, delete compulsions (e.g. nail biting), alter emotions, and many other things. By changing the submodalities, you will gain real control over your inner experience. You will learn to change your emotions in a few seconds, just like a swing of a magic wand. You will learn the structure of your thoughts and you will learn how to influence them.

Systems of Representation

Exercise time! Let's begin with a little experiment.

1. Sit back, close your eyes and remember a pleasant moment in your life. Get into this memory as deep as you can. With the eyes of your imagination, try to see all the things you saw then.
2. Add the sounds and hear what you could hear then. Touch something in this projection of yours, such as your clothes, and feel the material.
3. Then, imagine you're eating something (a lemon, for example), feel the smell and taste accompanying the representation.

As you have just experienced, the mind always thinks using exactly the same senses by which it receives and meets the outside world. That's why thinking can also be recognized as an internal process of using our senses. In neuro-linguistic programming (NLP), these senses are called "systems of representation".

Did you know that when you're imagining you're eating a lemon, exactly the same parts of your brain are being activated as if you were actually eating it?

The most common form of thinking is the internal dialogue, also called "the inner critic", or voice, be it ours or someone else's, which comments on all the events taking place in our reality. Your inner dialogue is the auditory system of representation. We'll go back to that in a moment.

Now, I want you to know that each of the senses by which we think has its own characteristics and properties. It's just as if you were watching television (perhaps using an old-school TV set), where you have various knobs under the screen. Using them, you can lighten or darken the image, adjust the color saturation, increase or decrease the sound volume and change the size of projected images.

All these parameters can be changed easily. **Exactly the same holds true when it comes to what you see, hear and feel in your own head**. In NLP, these parameters are called "submodalities". You can change them, thus controlling your thoughts, and therefore your life. Your mind is inextricably linked with the physiology of your body. Every thought immediately affects your emotional state, which, in turn, affects any behavior and decision in your life.

While working with submodalities, we mainly focus on three basic systems of representation: **visual, auditory and kinesthetic (sensory).**

The best way to understand any concept is to experience it, so **let's now do another exercise!**

How to Put Submodalities to Use

Close your eyes and bring back a memory—preferably the same one you worked with in the previous exercise. Give yourself a moment to remember exactly what you saw, heard and felt. When the overall representation of the experience is already clear, you can start having fun with submodalities. At the beginning, decrease the size of the image you see; then, go back and increase it.

Now, darken it significantly, only to make it very bright after a few seconds.

Then, move the image away from yourself as far as you can, so it shrinks to a little point somewhere on the horizon. After that, bring it back so close that it is right in front of your nose.

Let's now see how the auditory submodalities work. Reduce the volume of sounds occurring in your memory, and then increase them radically. Is anyone saying anything in this daydream? If so, increase the pace of the voice and make it higher, shriller.

Now, touch something and feel its temperature. Imagine this thing being very hot, then very cold.

You can now open your eyes.

You have just experienced having total control over your internal representations. You can do anything you want with them. Each image, regardless of whether it refers to your past or future, can be changed by you.

Anytime you cannot change the imagery of a particular submodality, just imagine there's a knob responsible for the given parameter just below the image. Start twiddling it, and you will see the representation is actually changing.

Benefits of Changing Your Submodalities

This "little trick" has huge implications in almost every area of your life:

- First of all, **you gain real control over your feelings.** It is your thoughts, images, and internal dialogues that evoke specific emotions. When you know how to change the parameters, with practice, you can change your emotions in a matter of seconds.

- **Better motivation**. Thoughts, in which you imagine something you just can't wait for, have different submodalities than the thoughts in which you don't feel like doing something at all. Check submodalities of the former, write them down on a piece of paper, and then modify the latter to have the same parameters.

- Working with submodalities is necessary to **get rid of unpleasant memories** from your past. By controlling the images that keep coming back to you, you can let go of all these emotions that keep haunting you. More on that later in this book.

- This also works the other way. As you imagine your future positively and in bright colors, you can buy into this vision even more, so your motivation to achieve your goals will be significantly stronger.

- What's more, the change of submodalities is the basis of work with the majority of neuro-linguistic programming techniques, which are one of the most effective ways to **create permanent change**.

To examine the first of these benefits in practice, let's do this little experiment now:

1. Bring back a memory that causes negative emotions in you. Once you imagine exactly what happened and you start feeling the emotions that accompanied this situation, begin to change the submodalities of your imagination. First of all, turn down the sound you hear there.
2. Now, make the image black and white and then make it darker. After that, make it smaller and start moving it away from you as far as possible. Make it a tiny point on the horizon. Now, check your emotions. What are you feeling? How has the modification of the submodalities changed your emotions?
3. Bring back a good experience, something you often enjoy returning to in your imagination or dreams. Get into this memory and start changing its submodalities. If you don't see the image from your own perspective, but from an observer's, change it and bring it to your own perspective. At the beginning, saturate the colors

and make them a little brighter. Now, magnify the image and zoom it in. Make it sharper and vivid. Then, make the sounds clearer and louder.

How do you feel now? What has the modification of submodalities changed in your emotions?

For most people, treatment with the example of a negative memory will contribute to the disappearance or lessening of the negative emotions, while treatment with an example of a positive memory with good feelings will intensify them.

There are people that are a walking exception to the rule, though. For these people, change in their submodalities may work differently. For some, which is rare, brightening an image might lessen emotions connected with a memory. All the other submodalities may work the other way around (or slightly differently), too. It is worth noting this is an individual matter and in different people, different submodalities can be crucial.

For one person, magnifying, or making an image larger, could make emotions much more intense, while for another, it wouldn't change anything. For the latter, distance, brightness, or loudness of an image may make a big difference.

I should also tell you more about one of the most important visual submodalities: association/dissociation. Every single image in your imagination you can see either from the perspective of your own eyes (exactly as you see the world right now), or from the observer's perspective (like watching a movie with yourself in the main role). The first option is association, when you are in association with your own experience. The second option is dissociation, when you see yourself in an image, from the third person's perspective. This submodality often plays a key role when it comes to the intensity of each emotion. For most people, association with an image increases the intensity.

This is why some unpleasant memories haunt you, when you see them in full association, colorful, large and clear. Now you know how to reduce their impact on your life. When you get rid of the emotional influence they bring along, they will finally disappear and never come back.

You can also do the opposite with positive memories, which can now provide you with a significant richness of pleasant emotions.

Here's the list of the most important submodalities:

- **Visual:**
  (in association/in dissociation)
  1. large/small
  2. frames/no frames
  3. near/far
  4. position/location of the image (where is it?)
  5. in color/black and white
  6. light/dark
  7. clear/fuzzy
  8. video (moving images)/static slide (single picture)
  9. three-dimensional/flat
  10. image shape: square/rectangular/round/etc.

- **Auditory:**
  1. source of the voice (where does it come from?)
  2. loud/quiet
  3. fast paced/slow paced
  4. high/low
  5. clear/unclear
  6. melodic/monotonous
  7. rhythmic/without rhythm
  8. clean/distorted (or echoed, etc.)

- **Kinesthetic:**
  1. intensity of touch or emotions

2. warm/cold
3. heavy/light
4. strong pressure/low pressure
5. smooth/rough

As an exercise, when you finish reading this chapter, you can check how each of these submodalities works for you. If you encounter any problems, e.g. with the change of temperature in your imagination, try the knob method. If this does not work, you can touch a warm radiator with your real hand, and then something cold a while later. Repeat it a few times. Then, close your eyes and just try to imagine you are doing the same thing, imagining the change of temperature.

You can do such things with every single submodality. This way you will master the total control over the images you create in your head. **This ability is an absolute basis for effective and lasting change, because your whole life is based on what you think and how you think.**

One very good idea might be to print a list of submodalities and then go through each of them, practicing from the first to the last position, until you feel you're doing better and better.

When I first started playing with submodalities, I found myself really surprised how easy and effective this tool was. It's been the basis for my work with emotions for a long time now.

For the "second course", I suggest you perform the following two exercises:

Strengthen Your Beliefs Using Submodalities

1. Select any conviction with which you have a problem believing and you're not sure if it is true, one you would like to enforce in yourself. For example, "*I can handle this task,*" "*I*

am strong emotionally," "*Quick learning is easy.*" This will be the belief you want to strengthen.

2. Find a statement or an experience from your life you are one hundred percent sure of. For example, "*The sun rises tomorrow,*" "*My name is...*" You must be absolutely sure this one is true.

3. Now, repeating the belief from the second step in your mind (the one you're certain of), close your eyes and see what kind of image is connected to it. Exactly specify the submodalities on a list. Write down whether the image is large or small, light or dark, near or far, etc. Pay attention to its specific location in space.

4. Then imagine your belief from the first point (the one you're doubtful about) and also specify all the submodalities. Again, note the location of this picture and all the other details.

5. With your eyes closed, still seeing the belief you want to change, start changing this picture's submodalities to make it look like the belief you were sure of. Let the image be exactly the same as in the beginning, just change its submodalities. All the parameters have to be the same as in the image you were certain of.

6. Having the changed image in front of you, what do you feel now? How has your perception of this belief changed? If you feel the change should be stronger, go through this exercise again. This time, try to concentrate a little bit more. Practice makes perfect.

Not only can your beliefs be enforced, but also changed entirely. You will read about it further in this book.

Get Rid of Stress Using Submodalities

Close your eyes and remember a stressful situation. Imagine how this stress looks inside of your body. Like a black dot? Like a heavy stone? Like a hot jelly? Look carefully, because soon you will get rid of it.

While doing this exercise, focus on your interior as much as you can and observe everything happening in your body. The emotion you're working with can look like anything—like a black orb, like shattered glass or raging flames. Be open to these experiences and write down every visual, auditory and kinesthetic detail of this emotion.

Here's how you do it:

1. Bring back any situation that usually makes you nervous/anxious/worried, etc. Make this vision detailed. See what you saw back then, hear what you heard, get into this as much as you can. Fully feel the emotion you want to get rid of. <u>Proceed to the next step only once you can really feel and experience it.</u>

2. Determine where exactly in your body you are feeling this emotion. Point to this place with your hand.

3. Now, describe how this emotion looks. First of all, think about its form—is it solid or liquid? Is it a gas? What is it exactly? You can use the list of submodalities from above.

4. Imagine you're grabbing this feeling with your hand and take it away from your body, putting it in front of you (you should really move your arm as if you were doing it). When the emotion's in front of you, it is not affecting you anymore.

5. Change every single submodality of this emotion to a submodality that fits you. The new form of this feeling has to be relaxing for you. You can change the temperature from hot to cool, color from red to blue, shape from sharp to ovoid, etc. Go through every single submodality, slowly and carefully changing it to the one you want.

6. As soon as you change all of the submodalities, look at this emotion again and ask yourself: is it the kind of emotion I want to have inside of my body? If so, proceed to the next step. If not, go back and change everything needing to be changed in this emotion.

7. Now grab this new feeling and put it inside your body, in the same spot where the old one was. Feel how pleasant it is settling there, relaxing all of your body. For a moment, imagine how the emotion resides there.

8. Again, imagine the stressful situation from the beginning of this exercise, this time with the new emotion you have created and observe how you're feeling.

Regarding step 4 — Sometimes you might have a problem with taking the emotion away. It can be hidden too deeply or have a form that makes it too difficult to grab.

No problem, here's a way to change that: imagine you have a tool in your hand that makes it easier, a knife, bucket, tongs or a vacuum cleaner, whatever. Use it to take the emotion out of your body in your imagination. Play with this process as much as you can, as it's completely about your imagination. Apply this technique frequently. With practice, you will learn how to do it very quickly, even without taking the emotion out of your body. You will just learn how to go through the process automatically.

Make this your goal for now, as making a habit out of this technique gives you extraordinary control over your emotions, which equals a considerable improvement in the quality of your life.

As soon as you're done reading this, go ahead and try this technique!

Chapter 6: Reframing

There's no such thing as a stressful or annoying situation. There's only your perception of each incident. **Some people give so much attention and meaning to various life events, they trigger emotions of stress or anxiety every single time.**

You can change the way you perceive reality quite easily, using a simple and effective technique, called "reframing". You will free yourself from many worries and will gain a deep peace of mind instead.

First of all, you have to understand that in every single eventuality, it is your mind giving meaning to the reality around you. Specific events, situations, behaviors or objects are never good or bad by definition, neither are they annoying or not annoying, stressful or relaxing. Every single time, it's YOU perceiving them that way, which is not always good for your emotional state.

Take rain, for instance. If you are going back home without an umbrella, a heavy shower won't be a nice experience for you. If you are a farmer experiencing six months of drought, the rain will be a salvation for you. If you live in an area endangered by frequent floods, rain could mean some serious trouble; but, if you were just to water your lawn, rain will save you some precious time. As you can see, rain is neither good nor bad by definition—it's the context and the way of perceiving it that gives the rain any attributes. It's the same case with anything else.

I want you to know you can change your perception of reality quite easily. By changing your point of view, you can instantly and entirely change your emotions connected with a certain situation or behavior of another human being. Thanks to this technique, you can control your emotions and choose whether you want to feel good or bad.

When someone close to you was supposed to call you three hours ago, but did not, you could think the person forgot about you and that you don't mean much to him/her. Such perception may make you angry and disappointed. What happens when you change the frame, which is the perception, and think of the possibility that this person's phone has broken? Your frustration will probably pass. What if the person had an accident and is now in the hospital? Not only will the anger pass, but also you will suddenly start worrying and caring about that person. As you can see, the change of frame causes an instant change of all your emotions.

I want to teach you how to interpret the events and behaviors you encounter in your everyday life, so it is beneficial for your emotional health. Metaphorically speaking, why would you worry if you can't really change the fact that it is raining? Why would you stress out, not even knowing the real reason beneath the lack of response from your friend, husband or crush? **So often, your mind just sees a tiny stretch of reality, interpreting it in a certain way.** There are always countless possibilities and explanations. You can **always** choose how to interpret a certain situation, which means you also have choice regarding your emotional state. Instead of stressing out, being angry or nervous, you can choose to be calm and relaxed. It will also allow you to make use of all your resources and faculties, which before your shift of perception, were covered by a dark cloud of negative emotions. There are two aspects of reframing: you can either change **context** or **content** of a given behavior or incident. I will expand on both of them in a moment.

Context Reframe

Context reframe is about asking yourself: **In what context would this behavior/situation be viewed as positive?** Rain is a very good example, as it can be viewed differently in various situations. In a context type of reframe you are looking for other situations, where a given event or behavior would be positive.

It will become clear to you when you read these examples.

Imagine your boss shouts at you at work, criticizing your behavior and your projects. You could get stressed out, but you have a choice. Think about it this way: maybe he is seriously sick and wants to discharge certain negative emotions? Or maybe he's going through some kind of family issues? Maybe his dad just passed? What if he wants to promote you and is now testing how you deal with difficult situations?

A few days ago, I heard a story about a woman who passionately runs an animal shelter in northern California. One guy told her, "*What's the point? You won't be able to save all these homeless animals living on the streets anyway!*" To which she replied, "*Imagine you are one of those hundreds in need... and it suddenly turns out that someone chooses you to help. From so many homeless, someone wants to save YOU. Would you say the same thing you just said a moment ago?*" Great reframe. The animal shelter owner put the man in a context in which he was the one in need. From this perspective, running an animal shelter looks totally different.

Context reframe also proves very useful when someone feels bad about a certain trait of their character. When someone's stubborn, which negatively affects contact with other people, they should also think that being stubborn is not always a bad thing. They will probably stubbornly seek to reach their goals. Distrust can be another example. Distrustful people sometimes have a hard time forming relationships with other people, but it's harder to lie to them, cheat them or take advantage of them. Depending on the point of view, every behavior can be favorable or unfavorable.

Content Reframe

Content reframe is about a change in perception of a given experience's makeup itself, which causes emotions in you. In this case, you ask yourself: **What can be another, positive meaning of this situation/behavior?**

You just missed your bus. What can be the pros of this situation? You will have a walk and some nice fresh air. It will be healthy, and you can step into a shop to buy yourself a tasty fresh fruit or a snack. Another example: you're late for an important meeting. You could be stressed about it, but why? When you walk in stressed, the kind of impression you make is much worse than the impression you would make when you walk in calm and steady. So you can reframe the situation; you could think that thanks to you being late you will be better remembered by other participants. You will make an entrance, which will make you stand out. Maybe you will miss a totally and utterly boring speech from one of your coworkers. As you can see, even being late could be quite a good thing!

Choose Wisely

Remember that Reframing is not about lying to yourself. You won't start lying because of reframing—you already have been lying to yourself! In fact, how you perceive a given situation very rarely has any reflection on actual reality. As I said before, you always see only a small stretch of reality. For instance, how do you know the boss yelling at you is a jerk, a yokel and he doesn't like you? All the other options detailed above (he's testing you as he wants to give you a promotion, he is seriously sick, etc.) are not any less possible, even if somebody told you your boss hates you.

There are very few things in this world that can be objectively observed (if at all, as some famous philosophers and quantum physicists say). With that being said, you have a choice on how to lie to yourself—so that you feel anger, frustration and stress, or so you feel calmness, relaxation and peace. **The choice is yours.**

Some time ago, I got stuck in a big traffic jam. All drivers were honking, throwing names and you could see lot of angry faces behind the wheels. In the meantime, I realized I would finally have the opportunity to listen to an audiobook I had on an old CD, for which I never had time whenever I was at home. It felt great, when others were drowning in seas of cortisol, a stress hormone over-stimulating neurons in their brains, I was relaxing and learning new things. Since I couldn't magically turn my car into a helicopter and escape the traffic jam, *Inspector Gadget* style, I had a simple choice: to stay in the traffic jam being nervous or to stay in it feeling good. I **chose** the latter.

My friend once told me a funny story. He was about to be operated on and put under anesthesia. Initially, when the doctor shared the news with him, he was very scared, but decided not to give away his control to this situation. He realized he had never before had the opportunity to experience the sensation of passing out into unconsciousness. Once he focused on this experience, he started feeling curiosity. "How will it feel when they put a mask on my face and I start falling asleep against my will?" He got so excited, he couldn't wait to get operated on, then felt really disappointed when the nurse told him the operation was going to be delayed. So much so, he actually had to reframe again—this time in the opposite direction, not to feel disappointment.

A Few Comments on Reframing:

1. Changing the way you perceive reality is a SKILL you can learn by constant training and practice, just like any other skill. Every time you come across a situation that is triggering anger or resentment inside of you—reframe it. **Practice changing your point of view and observe how it affects your emotions.** The more you practice, the easier it will be for you to reframe anything in the future. This way, you can choose emotions you want to have regarding both behaviors of other people, and unfortunate events you might come across.

2. Remember reframing doesn't have to be realistic and serious. So often, the funny and absurd things work the best. Try different things and see how your mind reacts to even the strangest and most unrealistic reframes.

3. Always choose the reframe that fits the best in a certain situation. Sometimes content reframe might prove more effective, whereas a different time context reframe might be more helpful. You will easily tell what's best for you in a given situation.

4. **Make reframing your new habit.** When you reframe often, you teach your mind it has a CHOICE how to perceive reality. When you practice changing your point of view frequently, reframing will grow into you. You will start doing it automatically, every time there's a negative emotion.

Practice this skill RIGHT NOW! Think of any events, past experiences, situations or behaviors (either yours or others') that you can reframe today.

Chapter 7: Is This Thought Real?

How many times have you been worried about something and then...it never happened? A few years ago, I worried a lot if I should quit my miserable job. "What if my business fails and I won't be able to find employment?" Then, I worried if I should move from my motherland to France to live with my girlfriend (I used to worry every time I wanted to move to some other place, and that was quite a lot). *"I don't speak French; Cote d'Azur is so expensive; what if my business goes downhill at that time; blah blah..."* Before then, I worried about whether or not I should finish my formal education, graduating with just a Bachelor of Arts, screw the Master's Degree, and find a well-paid physical job no one else wants to do for a short time, with the intention of saving up money to travel and chase my wildest dreams. Fortunately, I decided not to focus on my worries and I chose my happiness over my fears. I did what I wanted and never regretted it.

It turns out, more than 90% of situations people stress about never become real. Even if they do, they are certainly much easier to overcome than they would originally think. People create their own private hell that only exists in their minds.

Let me now show you one of the most effective, and yet simplest, methods to get rid of all thoughts that are the source of suffering and negative emotions.

Before you learn how to make use of this method, I will tell you about a few very important dynamics of your mind. At some point in your life, you have probably already noticed the vast majority of your worries never become real, and yet people regularly spend their days stressing and obsessing about everything and more. Therefore, they waste their lives and their present moments, exchanging them for their toxic, useless thoughts of various kinds.

As I said in the previous chapter, **your thoughts and reality are two different things!**

No matter what beliefs you have about this world, yourself or the people around you, they are not really consistent with reality. **EVERYTHING is your opinion on something,** which is a result of your perception of the whole world. Human reality is filtered through the prism of their experiences and beliefs, creating their own model of the world, uniquely individual for each person. **Remember, you never react for another human being or situation, you always react only as a result of your opinion about this person or a given event.**

Depending on whether your thought on something is positive or negative, either positive or negative emotions arise in your body.

It happens that lots of people in this world spend most of their time cultivating negative thoughts: *"John is impudent." "He has tricked me!" "She should be more inquisitive!" "I'm hopeless." "I'm too impulsive." "They are surely laughing at me." "People think I'm not smart enough to do this." "I won't pass this exam." "Learning new languages is difficult." "I have to be more self-confident." "They don't care about me."* So on and so forth. This, dear madam and sir, is utter horsecrap.

Every single one of these thoughts is nothing more than just your opinion about reality. **A little story in your mind that is not real**. It can't be objectively observed that learning languages is difficult, just as it can't be objectively observed whether, *"She should be more inquisitive,"* or not. Every single thought like that can be busted easily, which will take away its influence on your emotions.

Let me show you an example: imagine you broke your leg falling off a bike. You look at the blood, feel the pain... and suddenly the thoughts appear: *"I won't make it in this school," "People will start laughing at me," "I can't even ride a bike,"* and *"I will be in pain for the entire month!"* **Now, think for a moment—are these thoughts real?** In reality, it's just your mind's approach to what has just happened. What's the reality?

The reality is you've broken your leg falling off a bike.

End of story, period.

Everything else are additional impressions that just make you suffer. You usually don't react to reality, but to your thoughts about reality!

As long as you have various mind stories about the surrounding world, they trigger numerous emotions for a certain reason: **a thought can trigger suffering in you ONLY WHEN YOU BELIEVE IT IS TRUE.** However, when you stop believing in this thought, it stops affecting you. Thanks to some of the further techniques I'm going to present in this book, you will learn how to stop believing in your thoughts. This way you will get rid of all the unnecessary stress and anger in your life, and stop worrying about all the things that won't happen anyway.

Notice how often you are angry at someone, and then, in defense, that person reveals a new fact you never knew, which sets him/her in an entirely different light. For example, you might be mad at your friend who was to call you and never did. The next time you meet him, he explains his phone got stolen and he was beaten by some drunken hooligans. Now, all your anger is gone. Why? You just stopped believing in a thought you were certain of the whole time (*"He doesn't care about me at all"* or *"He's always forgetting about things"*).

It's enough for you to stop believing in all these mind stories that don't have anything in common with reality anyway, as this will cause the majority of your bad emotions to disappear.

Now, let me show you how.

Every Single Thought Comes with a Certain Consequence

Sometimes, even the thoughts and beliefs about the world that are seemingly positive can really be negative. For example, "Today is a good day as the weather is great!" This is a stick with two ends. Why? As soon as the beautiful weather is gone, the day will no longer be good, or even the opposite (*"The weather sucks! I just want to go to bed!"*). Why shouldn't it be good no matter what the weather is? It is therefore very important for you to deeply reflect on all your thoughts, beliefs and opinions, as every single one of them has an impact on your life and brings certain consequences. Depending on these consequences, you will either want to get rid of this thought or not.

Another example of mental stories worth working on are "mental duties". People so often judge that someone should've done something, someone should be more like this and that or something should or should not ever have happened. These thoughts always bring bad emotions, as they are results of resistance against what reality brings. Every single time you say "should" or "shouldn't", you are not accepting what's happening around you. **Why the heck would you resist reality, when you can't change it anyway?**

"Jacob shouldn't be so shy." This thought has two mental stories inside of it. Both have the ability to make you (and Jacob!) feel bad. The first one is *"Jacob is shy."* How do you know it is so? Maybe he is having a bad day? Maybe you are the only one who sees him that way? Notice how you will treat Jacob believing that he's shy. How would you treat him not believing your own story about him? The other story is *"Jacob shouldn't be shy."* Even if it is true, maybe he really needs it to learn something? Maybe he's good with being shy at this point in his life? Maybe he will close himself in a basement, invent a new startup and become the next millionaire, pushing this world forward thanks to his work? Also, the consequence of the thought that he shouldn't be shy is your conviction that Jacob will feel your lack of acceptance. Your pressure on the fact that Jacob should be different than he really is will just probably make him resist and feel reluctant. In the meantime, Jacob can also create a story about himself which goes, *"I'm shy..."* What kind of emotions will this thought trigger in him? Probably negative—and when Jacob is thinking that he's shy, he really becomes even shyer. Without this thought, he could feel more relaxed and start acting naturally.

As you can see, there's much more beneath the surface than you think. Having this knowledge, you will also start noticing more, which gives you big opportunities to grow and make your reality better.

The Work

The Work is a method that will help you get rid of any thought which brings you negative emotions. No matter if it's a thought about yourself, or about anyone else, about your past or your future.

The Work was created by Byron Katie, who fell into a very deep depression in her thirties. She remained in this state for more than ten years, when suddenly one morning she experienced the sudden glimmer. She understood something very important. Here's a quote from her book, <u>A Thousand Names for Joy</u>:

> "I discovered that when I believed in my thoughts, I was suffering, and when I did not believe them, I was not suffering... and that it applied to everyone else. Freedom is so simple. I discovered that suffering is a choice. I discovered the joy inside of me, which has never disappeared since then, even for a moment. This joy is present in everyone, all the time."

From then on, Byron Katie started to question every single thought that appeared in her mind. Although in reality, she wasn't the first one to come up with this kind of reflection or the first person to write about this kind of experience (you can read about very similar notions in the work of J. Krishnamurti, Rumi, Osho and Eckhart Tolle, also in ancient Buddhist scriptures and many reflections of Christian mystics), she came up with a very simple and effective idea, which now anyone can do the same. To cut a long story short, this method consists of **4 basic methods and inversions**:

1. Is this thought real?

2. Can you be 100% sure this thought is real?

3. How do you feel when you're thinking this thought?

4. Who would you be without this thought?

Inversion – invert the thought and then give three authentic reasons for which the new thought is real.

If you're entirely new to this method, I recommend you read this more detailed transcription of The Work below. You can rewrite and print the sheet, and it will make it much easier for you. You will also find notes to every step, which will help you understand the method better.

The Work is one of the most effective methods allowing a person to get rid of unwanted thoughts that I ever came across. It's worthwhile to spend some time on it—you will gain a tool that will accompany you for many long years. Let's do it!

The first stage preceding the four questions is called "rate your neighbor", and you will be filling it in only when the thought you are working on is about another person or about yourself. If it's a thought about some situation from the past, pass this step. Examples to help you understand each question are written down in italics. Also, there are notes cited in { } that then appear at the end of the form, to help you with filling out the form and answering questions you may have.

When you have all the info you need for beginning, start immediately! Print this form, write down a few thoughts or beliefs that cause negative emotions in you and start working on them.

Remember two very important concepts before beginning:

- Write down every answer on a sheet of paper. All of them! It will help you dissociate from the experience and will enable you to see your thoughts. Once they're written down on a piece of paper, you're moving away from them, which makes it much easier to work on them. It might often happen that you will be really surprised how you could have believed them at all, once you're finished with the process.

- Start with beliefs about other people! Only after you gain some experience, should you start working with beliefs about yourself.

"Rate Your Neighbor" Form

{SEE NOTE "A"} *Example: Ann is never listening to me.*

1. Who is the reason you are angry, confused, sad or disappointed, and why? What is it you don't like about that person?

I am...*angry*...**at**.........*Ann*.........**because**.........*she is never listening to me*.........

2. What kind of change would you want to see in that person? What do you want this person to do?

I want.......................*Ann to start listening to me*.......................

3. What should this person do or not do, think or not think, feel or not feel, be or not be? What kind of advice would you give to that person?

............*Ann*.........**should / should not**.........*listen to me carefully*.........

4. Is there anything you need from this person? What would it take for this person to make you happy?

I want...........*Ann to always listen to what I have to say* ......

5. What do you think about this person? Go for it, pour all your anger out on paper.

......*Ann*......**is**...........*an egoist, she only thinks about herself, she doesn't care about me at all*...........

6. What is it you don't want to experience again when it comes to that person?

I never want..............*Ann to treat me like that ever again*............

Now ask yourself these four questions:

1. Is this thought real? (yes/no)

2. Are you absolutely certain this thought is real? (yes/no)

If the answer is "no," proceed to question no. 3. If the answer is "yes" in both cases, use the steps below: **{SEE NOTE "B"}**

a) "Yes" means...what consequence results or what conclusion do you reach from thinking this thought? *(start working on the interpretation that will be built)*

Conclusion: I'm not important to Ann.

b) If you got what you wanted, what would happen? *(start working on what you would get)*

Would get: Ann would understand me better.

c) What's the worst case scenario? *(start working on the worst possible result)*

Worst Case: Ann will stop talking with me for good.

d) Add a duty. *(add "should/should've" and how to work on it)*

Duty: Ann should always listen to me and always let me know she's listening.

e) Find a reason, evidence to support the original thought. *(work with every single proof or evidence supporting your original thought, using the four questions to analyze each reason)*

Reasons/Evidence: Ann is never nodding when I talk to her. She is not looking into my eyes when I'm talking to her.

3. How are you feeling with this thought?

a. How are you feeling with this thought?

b. Does this thought bring peace or stress to your life?

c. What is happening in your body when you believe in this thought? What are your bodily reactions?

d. How does it affect your relations with other people? How do you treat them?

e. How do you treat yourself, thinking this thought?

f. What consequences does believing in this thought bring?

g. What bad thing do you think might happen if you stopped believing in this thought? (Make a list and go through the entire process again. **{SEE NOTE "C"}**)

h. Do you have any non-stressful reason to believe this thought? Do you want to get rid of this thought?

4. Who would you be without this thought? Close your eyes and think how would you feel without it?

Inversion/Reframing {SEE NOTE "D"}

Option 1: Invert this thought. Come up with a belief that is an opposite of the thought you are working on and find three authentic reasons to prove this new thought is real.

E.g.: Ann doesn't have to listen to me.

Option 2: Reframe this thought and refer it:

a) To the other side *(I'm the one not listening to Ann)*

b) To yourself *(I'm the one not really listening to myself)*

c) Invert totally *(Ann shouldn't listen to me)*

Lastly, find at least 3 reasons to prove each reframe is real. {SEE NOTE "E"}

NOTES

A. Once you're done with filling out the "rate your neighbor" form, pick a thought you want to work on. Sometimes it will be possible to pick a thought from the first step (e.g. *"I'm angry at Ann because she doesn't like me."* Then, you need to work on *"Ann doesn't like me."*). Sometimes not (e.g. *"I'm angry at Ann because she stole the money from my wallet."* If she has really stolen and that's the proven fact, you need to work on another step). Sometimes, you will be able to pick a thought from the further steps, especially the third one. Sometimes, it's worth it to choose more than one statement to work on.

B. It is extremely important for you to understand that the thought you're working on is not real. That's what the first two questions are for. None of these statements are real, but if you still think some of these thoughts are, use some of the options from below the second question. You can either choose a single one or all of them at once. Utilizing these options, you will get new "mind stories" on which you should start working from the beginning. When you work them through, using the entire process, go back to the original belief and ask yourself all these questions again, starting from the first step.

C. In the third step, *subsection g)* is the question about alternative benefits that can result from having faith in a certain belief. If you find out something bad really might result from that, then write down the answer to this question separately and go through the whole process again with the new belief. Go back and continue with the first belief, only once you're finished. For example, someone may believe that he's too skinny. Using the question from *subsection g)*, he might get an answer like, *"If I stop believing I'm too skinny, I will quit the gym and diet and get even scrawnier."* This belief is faulty (you can and you should go to the gym and keep your diet, without having bad thoughts about yourself), so he takes the belief and works on that one starting from the beginning. It is very important as you will see here:

All of your thoughts are interconnected. They are like a complicated structure or some kind of building. Some beliefs contain other beliefs, hidden somewhere underneath, which act as foundations to the first thoughts you began to work on. You will sometimes find them unexpectedly. You should then stop working on the stories you began with and shift your focus to these new ones. When you get rid of any of those freshly found beliefs, the original one you started with will probably collapse, as well. When you destroy a foundation, the whole building will fall. The same goes for your mind stories. For example, if you think, "I'm worthless" —this belief has its foundations. They could be such thoughts as: "I'm too fat to make friends," "I can't learn anything" or "I can't swim." If you just deal with "I'm worthless," you will get rid of this belief, but the foundations will still be there— nothing will change in the long run and the "I'm worthless" belief will regrow because the foundation for its growth was never handled and resolved. If you take care of stories like: "I'm too fat to make friends," "I can't learn anything," etc., then the whole structure will collapse. The belief "I'm worthless" will fall down by itself.

D. A brief note about the last stage of inversion—in this stage, you can choose the variant that suits you more, where variant no. 2 is both more accurate and effective. So if you're new to this, choose the second option.

E. Regarding the "three proofs"—they should be real and authentic, evidence you truly believe in. You can always find these, just look for them long enough until you find three. Every single belief, both positive and negative, can be proved in many ways. It's also a very good mind exercise.

Source: modified forms from various NLP message boards, also additionally edited by me to make it more effective according to my personal experiences.

Chapter 8: Empty Chair Technique

Let's now cover another highly effective technique.

Imagine yourself sitting in front of an empty chair. With your mind's eye, you can see the person you want to resolve a conflict with, or one with whom you want to just communicate better.

You start talking, then change the seats and take the role of the other person. That's the way in which you can solve part of your problems in relations with other people.

The inventor of this technique is Fritz Perls, the famous creator of *Gestalt* therapy (a therapeutic model created in the 1950's, focusing on what the client is experiencing here and now). As opposed to many therapies, the point of Gestalt is self-discovery through experiences and experiments. That's exactly what the technique I'm going to describe to you here is all about.

It's one of the most common techniques used to work on improving human relationships. It proves really effective when you don't know how to communicate with a person close to you. It's also great when: someone doesn't listen to you and you want to express your needs more clearly; you bear anger or resentment toward someone and you want to free yourself from this burden; you are stressed out before a job interview or audition; you are about to have an honest and important conversation with your partner and you're afraid of the situation; etc.

You can really use this technique to work on every single relationship in respect to many various situations. Healing relations is always about communication, and communication is the main field of interest here.

The Empty Chair Technique is a role-play. What's different—you are to play both roles. Instead of thinking about what might happen, you just play the role. Start communicating with the other person, alternately being yourself and then playing that person. You run a dialogue, always reacting to what you have said playing the previous role. What's the empty chair for? Why standing up and changing seats? Why play roles?

The built-in process allows you to connect with your natural reactions and emotions. You will release and express them in a safe environment (there's no risk of the other person judging you). The movement and change of place will allow you to separate yourself from your established ways of thinking. You will experience the situation almost as if you were experiencing it in reality.

Are you ready? Read the below instructions thoroughly:

Empty Chair Technique

1. Select a topic you want to work on using this technique. Think about the person that is relevant to the situation.

2. Set two chairs facing each other. Pick one and sit down.

3. Imagine there's that particular person sitting on the other chair. Imagine what that person is wearing, his/her facial expression and body language. Give yourself a moment to visualize this person as thoroughly as you can (you can close your eyes). If it's a hard thing to do, just try to feel this person's presence, smell, etc.

4. Think about your feelings towards this person. What would you want to communicate? What would you want to say? Express your feelings in an honest and direct way. You don't have to beat around the bush. If you want to shout, then shout. Express everything that's inside of you. Try not to judge the person, rather focus on expressing your own feelings. It might feel very awkward at the beginning, but DO IT! You should be alone in your room and maybe alone in your home/apartment, so you don't have to hold yourself back.

5. Stand up and sit on the other chair. Imagine you are the other person in the relationship. Consider how that person might react to your message. Now, playing that person's role, respond just as if you're continuing the dialogue. Don't think about it, just say it!

6. When you have expressed what you wanted to express, change the seats again. Continue the dialogue until "you two" say everything there was to say—so every emotion and opinion is expressed.

7. Write down your findings on a piece of paper.

As you can see, the technique is quite simple, at least when it comes to its description.

When it comes to doing it, that's not always the case. It all depends on the situation you have chosen to work on and the emotions inside of you. If there's one thing I am certain of, it's that going through the whole process thoroughly and carefully can result in extraordinary effects. I've taught this technique to many people, and numerous times I've seen big relief and readiness to cope with the situation in real life.

It was sometimes about expressing love to the other person, sometimes about communicating fear and doubts, sometimes it was about honest and difficult conversations. Playing roles in these situations is a great way to release all internal obstacles and deal with all the limiting emotions. When you become fluent in this technique, you can also use it for:

- working with emotions towards people no longer around us
- working on your internal conflicts, with your own sub-personalities (parts of your personality)
- direct work with your emotions (imagine you see a symbol representing this emotion, sitting on the opposing chair)
- preparing for different professional situations, such as conversation with your boss, your employee, negotiations etc.

You have just obtained all the knowledge needed to experience this technique in your own skin. Now, all you need is a pair of chairs. You can, of course, postpone it, but now is the best moment to do it. It will take you no longer than 10 minutes. **As soon as you get finished, remember to write down your reflections on a piece of paper! You may be surprised.**

Chapter 9: The Nine Things You Need to Stop Doing to Yourself

The way to emotional happiness and freedom doesn't always require gaining new skills. Very often, the key to solving your problems is to quit some behaviors and kill habits that limit access to your inner energy.

When you eliminate what holds you back, you get to touch your real nature, not intoxicated with detrimental patterns. Let's now talk about ten things you should stop doing, starting today!

1. Stop pretending you are someone you are not.

What's the point in making up artificial personalities, when they're just fake, fleeting illusions? Even if someone "buys" what you're trying to sell, their opinion won't be about you, but about the artificial creation you made up. **Being yourself is one of the biggest challenges in life.** One of the main reasons for that is the fact that the media and our society inflict pressure on you to fulfill their expectations. **The only expectation you should have is to feel good in your own skin.** It is not an accident that the people receiving the most attention, respect and love are the people who are the most authentic and real. To put it directly, these are the people who don't give a flip about the roles society wants them to fit in and they follow their own set of values. You need to be yourself, your BEST self.

2. Stop lying to yourself.

You can never succeed in this shady practice, anyway. Somewhere deep inside, you will know the real truth. Lying to yourself gives short-term relief and a possibility to escape from your problems. In the long run, it only creates mental damage and conflicts between the sub-personalities you've created. **Be real for yourself** and never be afraid to tell yourself the whole truth, even if it's not convenient or easy. This will build a strong and reliable relationship with yourself, which is an extremely important foundation of self-worth. There's an old Russian proverb which goes, "*Better to be slapped with the truth, than be kissed with a lie.*" I couldn't agree more.

3. Stop focusing on what you don't want in your life.

If I was to share with you only one truth about this world of which I'm 100% sure, I'd say: **you get what you give.** Your thoughts and emotions are a form of energy you send out. It always returns to you, sometimes in some other, seemingly unrelated life situations. If you focus on destructive thoughts and emotions, you will often come across destructive events and behaviors. If you start focusing on the positives in your life instead, and start creating the positive energy within, you will see reality in bright colors. Don't ask me if it's the "Law of attraction", "Law of Karma" or any other such thing, because the name is the least important thing here. Hundreds of life experiences and "coincidences" have proven to me this is real, but also the expertise of many quantum physics researchers is enough proof for me. Even if I'm somehow wrong and delusional, you should Google search and read about the "self-fulfilling prophecy", a really interesting sociological phenomenon coined by Robert K. Merton. In short: the predictions you make about the future will, either directly or indirectly, cause themselves to become true, due to your feedback between your predictions and your behavior. I'm not being spiritual now. It's neurobiology. It's about how our brains work. Look it up. See—not only is focusing on the negatives ineffective, it is also dangerous, and therefore simply stupid. The same goes to your use of language. Every time you say you are tired or angry or stupid, it is very possible you will start feeling or acting so. Every single word in your dictionary has already been anchored to a certain emotional state, so be very careful here. Some words and statements will help you, while others will hold you back and harm you. Focusing on what you want is in your best interest, every single time.

4. Stop giving your needs the lowest priority!

You don't know how to take care of yourself, yet you'd like to take care of other people?! YOU are the most important person in your life and it's the high time for you to become fully comfortable with this thought! Human beings are biologically programmed to care about their own butts in the first place. Unfortunately, this trait is being displaced by our "political correctness" sheep flock society, and being called "selfishness", which causes remorse every time we want to fully focus on ourselves.

In result, we are almost constantly looking for other people's approval and expecting people to take care of us. TAKE CARE OF YOURSELF FIRST! That's another crucial foundation of self-esteem and self-worth. Then, and only then, will you really be able to take care of others in the long run. Only a good relationship with yourself will give you the power to deal with other people's problems and the ability to truly take care of them.

5. Stop wasting your time on all the things that DON'T MATTER!

Are all the things you do every day, either at work or after, important to you? If not—CUT THEM OFF. The time you have left on this planet is rather limited, so start holding dear every single minute of your day. Don't make the assumption you will stick to your work now so you will have more free time in the future—your life is **here and now.** If you can't appreciate it today, why would you assume that will change in the future? I will repeat— **you are living your life RIGHT NOW. There's no other life in this reality.** Define what's important to you and don't allow yourself to waste your time on things of little importance! Would you willingly throw you money away to the gutter? Don't do the same to your minutes. They can never be earned back.

6. Stop blaming yourself and others for your problems.

Shifting the responsibility onto other people is very convenient, but at the same time, this trick is a treacherous trap. When you don't have the responsibility, you don't have the control. When you're devoid of control, you become helpless and expect others to take care of your problems and solve them for you. If something shows up as a problem to you, it is because you are perceiving it that way. Usually it's no one's fault, not even yours (even if it was, that doesn't matter at all). Accept it as an actual state of things and take the responsibility for what is happening. Reclaim your control and think what YOU can DO to change it.

7. Stop proving your value to others (but don't stop providing value).

The need to constantly prove to others you are a man of value shows you are not really sure of that. Don't waste your energy on the showoff behaviors, when you can direct the same energy inside yourself. It will allow you to focus on building a strong relationship with yourself and a strong sense of self-worth. Once you achieve it, the constant need for showing others how funny, sociable, self-confident and cool you are disappears completely. Then, you have more time and energy to achieve your goals and provide the real value.

8. Stop spending your time with people you don't want to spend your time with!

There's a possibility you have some people in your social circle who smother your positive attitude towards life, slow you down and make you feel worse. Don't maintain your relationship with them just because *"Fate brought us together,"* or *"I'm so used to hanging out with them."* You then feel uncomfortable quitting those relationships. Instead, hang around people who help you be the person you are when you are at your best. Making new, healthier relationships doesn't have to be time consuming or difficult, and it will probably prove to be a great source of joy and unrestrained self-development.

A Short and Simple Exercise.

Make a list of your friends, coworkers and people you sometimes hang out with. Think deeply and honestly, which emotions are the most frequent in these people? Positive or negative? How does it make you feel? How does it influence your emotions, your relationships with these people, and with other people?

9. **Stop running away from your problems. Start asking yourself the right questions, instead.**

The problems will be back anyway, if you don't take care of them. Running away from them is not the smartest way to make your life any better. Instead, take some time to reflect on your current life challenges and think about possible solutions. Write your problem on a piece of paper, and start asking yourself questions regarding what you can really do to solve the problem. In many cases, it won't be easy, but the bigger your challenge, the bigger lesson and self-confidence you will learn when you accomplish it. It won't always be possible to solve your problems right away, but the fact alone of getting familiar with them will make a big difference. Not everyone knows how to ask themselves the right questions to lead to concrete solutions.

I will expand on this area in the following chapter.

Chapter 10: The Lost Art of Asking Crucial Questions

The very essence of asking yourself questions is... to hear the answers. Usually, when you ask a question, the answer comes to you naturally and enables you to consciously look for new solutions. However, sometimes you ask yourself a question, just to find yourself in complete silence. What do you do then?

Be patient. Since the answers always come from within, you have to turn all attention to it and patiently wait, carefully observing your stream of awareness. One very good thing to do is to close your eyes and clear your mind from all excessive thoughts. You could definitely use a short meditation session.

Then, when you're calm, focused and relaxed, ask yourself this question again and wait for the answer. It can show up either as an internal voice, or an image appearing in your head. It can also be a remembrance of some other memory, a symbol, sound or a premonition.

If the answer still hasn't shown up, you can also ask yourself the question again, but this time use a slightly different form.

Before you ask yourself a couple of important questions, remember these two things:

- **You need to write down your answers.** Thanks to this, you will free your mind from thinking about all the solutions you have just come up with, and you will give it some extra space to look for the new answers.
- You don't have to write down all of the answers word for word; you can just use the keywords.
- **Start your questions with "HOW," not with "WHY."** The first type of question generates solutions. The second one only explains the situation you've already found yourself in. In most instances, the "why" questions won't be too helpful, whereas by thinking about HOW you can change your situation, you will eventually find the ideas you need.

Before the end of this paragraph, let's practice a little bit. As you have read the paragraph above, you've probably found yourself asking some questions already. If that's the case, let yourself fully ask these questions and see what you get. You can also use my help. Below you will find a list of some very useful and clever questions. Ask them yourself one by one and take the parts you need of what appears in the response.

- What can I do to feel better?
- How can the knowledge I've just obtained (when reading this book, or any other) be practically incorporated into my life?
- What can I learn from this person? (Before having a conversation with someone.)
- What can I do to achieve my dreams even faster?
- What's one new thing I can try or do today for the first time?
- How can I increase my income?
- If I was guaranteed to be receiving a lifetime salary high enough to live abundantly, what would I commit to? What would be my passion, hobby, business and lifestyle?
- What can I learn from this situation?
- What have I learned today?
- How can I turn this situation in my favor?
- If I was to be alive for only one more month, what crazy things would I do?
- How can I make other people feel better around me?

So often one single question is far more valuable than countless hours of explanations and convincing. The truth is unless you come to a certain realization yourself, there's no way anyone can help you. So often, you need to "wake up" and see your life and actions from another perspective, to start thinking independently and thus be able to discover important things about yourself to change the way you see reality. That's why people calling themselves "life coaches" so often fail. People usually shift the responsibility to change from themselves to these coaches. In reality, you are the only person who can really "coach" yourself. Coaches and therapists often know the right method, but you are the one to pull the trigger and do the real work.

Another set of questions below will help you with that:

- **"What do you want to have instead?"**

  That's a great question to ask yourself any time you focus on the things you don't want in life. It's extremely important not to focus on a problem, but on a solution. This question will shift your focus. The ability to control your attention is crucial to achieve effective and lasting change in your life.

  Every time your mind goes, "*I don't want to feel awkward when talking to freshly met people,*" instantly ask yourself, "*What do you want instead?*" You will usually get an answer like, "*I want to feel calm and relaxed to be able to enjoy the conversation.*" That's the answer you are looking for—a **positively stated objective.** People so often focus on what they don't want, instead of what they want; it's really hard to believe.

  Interestingly, since most people are not used to thinking that way, it proves to be a huge challenge for them.

  You have to carefully listen to your own answers, because even when you start thinking about your goal/objective positively and proactively, it can take as little as a few seconds for you to go back to the old model of thinking. You should then remind yourself about the question again, having in mind that you should focus on your goal, not on the obstacles. Remember, if you are looking for obstacles, you will always find them in abundance. They will keep growing in your mind.

- **"How will you feel once you achieve your goal?"**

  The role of this question is to experience a reality in which the problem doesn't exist anymore. It's the continuation of the process started in the first question. It's not only important for you to establish typically rational references (which usually arise thanks to the question from the first point), but also **emotional references.** It's also worthwhile to extend your answer: for example, if you think you will feel calm, you should ask, "What's calmness to you? How do you perceive it?"

This way you allow yourself to feel emotions coming from living a life in the world without this certain problem. You should also observe your body language and posture. If, for instance, you stand tall instead of slouching after asking yourself these questions, you are certainly on a good path.

- **"If you knew, what would it be?"**

  This question falls into the so-called "as if" frame category. So often, you won't be able to respond to some of the questions that will arise. For instance, if you ask *"What stops me from feeling better?"* The answer could just be, *"I have no idea!"*

  Still, there's a huge possibility you know the answer and it lies somewhere in the deeper levels of your consciousness, to which you don't have direct access.

  If you ask yourself this question, in most cases it turns out that usually something comes to your mind then. Often, it's an accurate answer. You can use this question: *"Indeed, it's not easy to find an answer to such a complicated question, but if I knew, what would it be?"*

- **"If you knew that you couldn't fail, what would you do?"**

  When you are being held back by the fear of failure, you will have a hard time accessing rich behaviors and making meaningful decisions. This question enables you to put the fear aside for a moment, allowing you to reflect on the actions you would take if you weren't so afraid of failing. A little injection of positive emotions and stepping outside the problem will surely make it easier to overcome your limitations.

So often, your answers to these questions will come as a practical action which you always wanted to take, but never had enough courage. For instance: *"I'd start my own company, instead;" "I'd go abroad;"* or *"I'd go talk to that girl."* That's very important feedback to have.

- **"What are you like when you are your best self?"**

This question allows you to quickly gain access to the resources which have been hidden behind some limitations. Starting from a point where you can access the positive states and beliefs makes it easier to deal with the issues you want to overcome. Answering this question, you might say things like, *"I feel totally free,"* or *"I feel powerful."* Remember them and all the emotions connected to them, because they might be the key to accessing your preferred emotional state.

- **"Do you think something bad can happen once you get rid of the problem?"**

I know—this question looks ridiculous. It's probably totally useless and I just ran out of meaningful ideas, right?

Wrong!

So often, people benefit from the situation in which they are having a certain problem! Those benefits can be wrapped around numerous things: such as family or a partner taking care of that person when they feel sick; increased social attention because they feel bad and deserve a pat on the back from their friends and some comforting talks; or faster "ending" of conflicts, when someone uses force and abusive behavior. When you were a little kid and you started crying, what happened? Your parents ran to you and gave you loads of hugs, kisses, comfort and attention. You got a prize for your sulking. Maybe they sung you a song or gave you some warm milk. This behavior is literally hardwired into our brains.

Unless the person finds an alternative way to fulfill these positive intentions, it will be really hard to get rid of the unwanted behavior. In this case that would be, respectively, fulfilling the need to be loved, being noticed and resolving conflicts.

So, when you obtain any alternative benefits coming from the preservation of a specific problem, you can do two things: first of all, change your belief that things, such as shouting, are a good method of building authority in relationships (more on changing your beliefs later in this book); second, provide yourself with alternative solutions to achieve your goal.

- **"Once you obtain 'X', what will be your benefit?"**

This question is a great way to find the most important values driving your motivation to achieve a certain goal. That's the thing Tony Robbins was talking about in his famous speech, "Why we do what we do?"

> Once your mind says, "*I want to finally get promoted!*"
>
> Ask yourself, "*Once you get your promotion, what will be your benefit?*"
>
> Answer, "*My salary will be bigger.*"
>
> Question then becomes, "*Once you have more money, what does it change? Why do you need that?*"

Going further down that path, you could obtain information that the money will give you the opportunity to go for a holiday wherever and whenever you want to go, which gives you the feeling of freedom. The information about "freedom" will serve you as priceless data! Notice that someone else could have entirely different motivations connected with promotion—for example, a feeling of power coming from being higher in the hierarchy. If you want more freedom, maybe you should think about starting your own business instead or becoming a freelancer? And so it goes.

- **"What blocks/stops you?"**

This is a question worth asking any time you hear yourself saying, *"Something is blocking me,"* or *"Something is holding me back from doing that"*. That's important information for you—you are putting the blame on "something".

It is not too helpful when you want to get rid of that block, as it fools your consciousness into believing the obstacle is something external, which implies limited control.

The questions, *"How do I block myself?"* or *"What exactly makes me feel blocked?"* bring the responsibility back to the table. It turns the noun "obstacle" into the process of "blocking". **It's easier to stop an ongoing process, than to get rid of already established things, especially things that are external. Sometimes, the devil's in the details.**

- **"How does 'A' cause 'B'?"**

> *"His sophisticated way of saying things makes me irritated!"*
>
> *"Why does it make me irritated?"*
>
> *"Because it makes me think I'm less educated and thus worse than he is..."*

Bullseye! One simple question and you know which way to go.

We are often victims to this structure of "A causes B," where many unrealized beliefs are hidden. In this case, it's, *"I'm worse than he is."*

If you were to begin from working on the emotion of irritation alone, you could have never found this important belief.

You could go further and ask, "*How exactly is it that all these sophisticated words he is constantly using make me worse than he is?*" Maybe you would get an answer like, "*Because it shows me I don't have the faintest idea about so many things.*" Then, here comes another belief you should change: "*Every time I don't know something, I'm a worse person than (other person).*" Then, when you have changed it, take action to learn more.

All these questions from the above are tools I encourage you to **test regularly and constantly. Once you have learned when to use each of these questions,** you will be able to trigger fast changes in your thinking and emotions.

Write all these questions from this chapter on a piece of paper, **learn them by heart, and think of which situations would best make use of these questions.**

Chapter 11: How to Deal with Internal Dialogues

Now, this is huge—stop telling yourself unpleasant things! Would you say these things to someone you respect or love? *"You can't do that," "You are stupid,"* or *"It's not going to happen."* So, why the hell are you telling them to yourself?

Listen carefully to your internal dialogues and check what it is you're saying to yourself every single day. Are these words positive, supporting and uplifting, or rather criticizing, reproving and unpleasant? It turns out that often the biggest obstacles to human beings are themselves. You should make your inner critic your best friend. To make your relationship with yourself better, you can start it over. Begin by saying "Hello!" with a big smile on your face and the proposition of spending a happy and joyful day together.

On that note, let me now expand a little bit on the art of dealing with internal dialogues.

NLP enables you to change your emotional state in just a matter of seconds. The best way is to change your (often vicious) internal dialogues, which so often contribute to the formation of stress or lack/decline of motivation.

Fortunately, you can rein over this grumpy laggard and transform it into an assisting and encouraging servant.

For people that don't control their internal dialogue, it is a tireless commentator on everything that happens around them. It is constantly commenting on people they meet (their look, behavior, statements) and events they are taking a part in. It also comments on your ideas (or lack of them) and actions (or lack of actions) and is always expressing opinion on them.

Do you have such a voice? If so, are you identifying yourself with it? Do you think that YOU are the voice?

Think about this.

In reality, **you are not your internal dialogue.** It is just a product of your imagination, formed in the process of evolution, which has accompanied mankind since we learned how to use languages.

Everything would be cool if not for the fact that most people in this world don't even realize they are constantly and pointlessly babbling to themselves! It's because they can't control their internal dialogue at all... and it has crucial influence on how we feel. The content of what this critic says to us, and also various tones of this inner voice, can change our emotional state in a few seconds.

What are your internal dialogues like? Is the depressing voice in your head saying, *"Great, another f**** day in the school/office,"* every morning? Or maybe, *"I'm so thankful to be alive for another morning, let's make this day a great one!"*

When you are about to accept a challenge, is the voice saying, *"I'm not going to make it anyway, it makes no sense..."* or is it saying, *"I will crush it! I can't wait to do that!"*

Your internal dialogues define the quality of your life. It depends on them whether you are bored or having a blast. You can make a great change in how you live by just changing how and what you are saying to yourself in your mind.

Before you start changing your internal dialogues, it would be great to set your ears to what is going on inside of your head. **The awareness of thought processes happening in there is the very first step to any self-change.** Close your eyes and imagine yourself in different life situations. Pick a few ones important to you, e.g. a first date with your crush, first day in a new job, accepting a new challenge, starting in a competition, thinking about your life goals, self-assessment, preparing for exams, etc. Exactly imagine yourself in these situations and listen to what are you then saying to yourself. What are the exact words you use when you are thinking about that and what are you doing in these contexts? When your internal voice is telling you things, what tone of voice does it have? What emotions do you feel because of all that?

Since you are now aware of the way your internal critic is communicating with you, you can start playing around with its modification. Any time you change anything, carefully observe how it is affecting your mood and emotions. **Even the slightest change in your internal dialogue can significantly impact the way you feel**. Therefore, the effects will certainly be very clear.

Let me now show you the seven most effective ways to claim control over your more or less "mean" internal dialogues. Using each of these ideas, every time pick a different context in which you are saying particular things to yourself. Process most of your internal dialogues this way and your everyday emotions will change significantly. Let's do it now!

1.   In the beginning, realize why the internal voice is saying anything at all. In other words, **discover the intent of your internal critic.** Ask it, *"What do you want to achieve by doing this? What's your point when you're saying that?"* You will usually get the answers instantly, and you will often realize the intent of your internal dialogue is truly positive. Sometimes, it will be the willingness to provide you with safety, to avoid failure or to motivate you to action. Once you know what the purpose was, thank your internal voice for that and it will let it go. The awareness of this intent will let you understand the goal of your inner critic without discouraging yourself.

2.   Every time you identify any particular sentence brought and repeated by your inner critic that gives you bad emotions (e.g. *"You will never amount to anything,"* or *"You don't deserve to be happy"*), do this: say the same sentence to yourself in your head, but now make two seconds break between every word. Say the words normally, just insert a two second pause in between all of them. See how it changes the emotions associated with the internal dialogue. This little trick breaks the pattern, causing the message to lose its emotional burden. After that, take the next step and tell yourself the same thing with four seconds break between the words. How are you feeling?

3.   **Change the tone, volume, pace and other sub-modalities (parameters) of your dialogue.** See how a silent whisper, increased tempo or bored tone work for you. If you want to get rid of negative

emotions, see what happens when you are decrease the intensity of the dialogue. If you want to empower the positive dialogues, do the opposite. Test different variants and observe your emotions with your eyes closed. You can also entirely change your internal dialogues, giving them the voice of Mickey Mouse, Darth Vader or anything/anyone else. Play around with this process, and once you find the most helpful and effective combinations of different parameters, remember them and use them as frequently as you can.

4.   This might be a little bit offensive and vulgar to some people, so excuse me in advance, but also believe me when I say that it works great. What wouldn't you do for comfort and peace of mind? Richard Bandler, the creator of NLP, once said he had a special mantra he used every time when his internal dialogues were getting too annoying.

This mantra is: **"SHUT THE F*** UP!!"** and you should repeat it a few times, until your internal critic...well, shuts the f*** up. I often use it when my mind starts acting like a little cowardly boy, hiding beneath his mom's apron. Any time my internal voice acts whiney and tries to bomb my decisions and actions with stupid excuses and doubts (*"But why go to gym? It's so far away from home and I gain muscle so slowly anyway... Why learn new languages, almost everyone in the world speaks English, blah-blah-blah..."*), I grab its neck and push it to the ground. It's my internal voice that serves me, not the other way around.

5.   When you are thinking about your goals and milestones, **play the music that motivates you.** It should be any energetic tune that triggers the feeling of unlimited motivation inside of you. You can look for such pieces in war, fantasy or adventure movies, for example. You could also use classical music. When you are setting your goals and planning things with this kind of music, your internal dialogues will be entirely different.

6.   In negative dialogues, **put the emphasis on a different part of the sentence to make it sound like a question**. Such intonation defines the sentence as questionable, which makes the negative aspect go away. In positive

dialogues, make it sound like an order. It empowers the emotional message and makes you feel better.

7.   **Practice the externalization of internal dialogues.** In other words, start saying aloud all the things you are thinking (okay, maybe not necessarily when other people are around). Think loudly. This exercise will give you the awareness of your internal dialogues and, quite possibly, you will be really surprised by what you will hear. It will also be a changing experience as you will realize what kind of chaos rules in your head so often. You can go all out and decide to externalize your dialogues entirely in every context, for a certain amount of time (the reactions of people passing you by on the streets or waiting with you in the line at the bank can really be diverse), or only when you are alone. There is also another variant of this exercise, which I personally have found really useful—instead of saying your internal dialogues aloud, you can write them down in a journal. In will help you take a step back from them, see them from a distance, and thus gain a deeper insight.

Test the above ways of dealing with your internal critic and experience how easily you can change your emotions. Add your favorite ways from above to your list of mind tools and let them serve you by giving you freedom, peace and joy in every moment of life.

You should also realize, in some situations and contexts, the internal dialogues in your head, or the so-called "internal critic", can be really helpful. For example, if you "don't feel" like going to the gym because it's raining and blah-blah-blah whatnot, your internal critic can often act as a whip to help you move your butt from the couch, stop whining like a little puppy and take the right action towards your goals! You have to take that into consideration and sometimes allow your internal dialogues to criticize you, push you and make yourself a little bit uneasy.

All you need to do is realize which dialogues and thoughts help you, and which hold you back. Then, empower your allies and annihilate your enemies. In some life situations, make your inner voice even stronger to keep yourself together.

Chapter 12: Internal Conflicts Troubleshooting

The human mind is often full of absurd contradictions. These internal conflicts are a significant obstacle in the way of achieving our goals. Fortunately, our subconscious parts (from which one could desire to eat a piece of delicious cake and another to lose a few pounds) can be integrated in order to harmoniously resolve the conflict.

The integration allows you to get rid of many internal conflicts and doubts. By having a chat with your subconscious, you can come to an agreement with two contradictory parts, which in turn will give you a strong feeling of integrity. You will change your emotions and release your energy to take action.

"Part" is a metaphorical term for a set of certain beliefs and attitudes, which bind to the specific emotional anchors and specific behaviors. Parts are usually subconscious, which simply means you don't know they exist. Using the "parts scheme" allows you to quite easily "catch" the part of your mind responsible for a certain problem and effectively solve the issue. This model simply treats some fragments of your personality as separate parts, which guided by certain intentions, produce the outcome that isn't always really desired by you.

I'm sure numerous times you have had the impression that one part of yourself wants to achieve something, while another wants something completely opposite, as if you were internally torn or hosted two different people inside of your body.

There are lots of beliefs, intentions, emotions and desires in your body and mind that you have never realized before, but they are constantly affecting your daily decisions and actions. What would you say for a little exploration that could significantly change your approach to certain things and even remove some unwanted behaviors and actions?

Many of you have never had a chance to dive inside your personality as deep as you will with this technique.

The conflict between parts is usually about the contradiction of your own beliefs that you have internalized (took as true). It turns out it is possible to have two different opposite beliefs at the same time! For instance: you can believe both that, *"It's worth it to eat sweets,"* and *"Eating sweets is not worth it!"* It all depends on what is behind this "worth" and "not worth"; that is, what is the purpose of eating or not eating the sweets.

Each part has a specific purpose of existence. For example, you can feel pleasure and relax when you eat sweets. When you don't eat them, you can achieve a slim figure and feel more attractive. This quite popular internal conflict creates lots of doubt in many people as soon as they reach for a donut or a piece of Christmas cake.

This subconscious squabble has results you are probably already familiar with. Two internal dialogues appear. One of them says, *"Ummm, this looks really delicious. I will only take one piece..."* The other one tries to convince you, *"I don't know about it, doesn't look like a good idea... I don't want to be fat, so I guess I will skip it..."* Internal contradictions are able to make even the simplest decisions really difficult.

Take a look at the examples of other popular internal conflicts:

- I want to exercise, go to the gym and run for a while. <-> I want to stay at home and finally relax.
- I want to go party with my friends. <-> I want to spend a calm evening at home and watch a movie or read a book.
- I want to have a road trip with my friends and leave the city for a weekend. <-> I want to study for an upcoming exam.
- I don't want to take risks, so I will keep my fulltime job at the office. <-> I want to go abroad and chase my dreams.
- I want to keep my diet and go to the gym regularly to gain muscle. <-> I want to go for a low-budget backpacking trip in Africa for five months.

At first sight, it looks like a challenge to reconcile two conflicting parts, but it's much easier than it appears. You can negotiate with them an agreement which makes them cooperate and support your decisions and actions.

This internal congruence will increase your self-confidence and help you achieve your goals. I'm about to show you a method that will help your resolve your internal conflicts and contradictions.

It is very important to recognize there's something more besides your fundamental internal objectives. This "something" is called a "meta-objective", which means a higher level goal. A meta-objective is an answer to the question, **"What's the purpose of achieving this goal?"**

For example, the meta-objective for achieving pleasure by eating sweets could be a feeling of joy, and on the higher level happiness. Whereas, the meta-objective for achieving a fit body could be attractiveness, and on higher levels: sex-appeal -> acceptance from significant others -> self-acceptance -> happiness.

As you see, happiness is the final goal in both cases and you should know the majority of seemingly contradictory internal conflicts **have identical meta-objectives.** The only tool you need to discover your meta-objective is the question to ask yourself: *"What's the final the purpose of achieving this goal?"*

For instance, what's the purpose of not eating sweets and highly processed foods? Fit body and good health. What's the purpose of having a fit body and good health? You will look attractive. What does looking attractively change? You're probably going to be more self-confident and more successful with other men/women. And so on, until you reach the point that leads to no further answer to the question.

The identification of the final goals above is the core of the process which I'm giving you below. It's a chain of goals method designed to help you integrate contradictory parts, based on making internal negotiations. Every time you discover an internal conflict in yourself, take these steps:

1. **Pick a behavior.** It could be a goal that raises your doubts, certain behavior that isn't congruent with your values, or simply a matter which makes you feel "torn".

2. **Identify the parts.** Identify the part of yourself which causes negative behavior, and also the part that is resisting this behavior. Name the parts with one word or one sentence, and write it down on a piece of paper or index card. Examples: "party-animal" and "couch-potato", "foodie" and "health-conscious", "safety-seeker" and "risk-taker".

3. **Specify the fundamental internal objectives of each part.** Think deeply, what does each of them want to achieve? Remember you are looking for a positive intention—what benefits do each part want to get you by its existence? Sometimes, these benefits can be hidden a little bit, but they are always there. You can ask yourself a question like, *"What do I gain or obtain by staying home instead of going to a party?"* The answer could be safety, time for yourself, relaxation, time to build your business, etc. Write down the fundamental objective as soon as you find it.

4. **Identify meta-objectives.** What is the positive outcome you want to gain trough the pursuit of the fundamental objective you have found in step three? What's the specific reason of achieving this goal? By gaining more time for yourself, do you get the possibility of achieving your personal goals? What exactly is the purpose of achieving them? Ask yourself these questions until you get to the higher ultimate goal, beyond which it's impossible to find more answers. Write down all the answers on the sheet of paper!

5. **Negotiate an agreement and get to the settlement.** Explain to your inner parts how they disturb each other on the way to achieving their, often common, goals. How do they hold each other back? Then, negotiate the agreement by asking, *"If one part agrees to refrain from harming you, will you refrain from stopping that part?"* Wait until an answer comes (either in form of internal dialogue or a feeling), and if there's still a need, keep negotiating. Be a mediator between two parts. Think how they can reach their goals alternatively and find a solution that will be satisfactory for both parts. Speak to your parts and get to the final settlement.

6. **Propose a trial period.** It will be a time when both parts will be working together. Propose a week of trial cooperation. During that time, keep observing the effects of the settlement.

7. **Check the results.** After a few days, see what has changed in the context of this specific matter. If there's still a need to do so, negotiate once again and propose the trial period for another time.

I KNOW this method may seem strange, quirky or maybe even creepy to some of you (like playing a guy with split personality, Hitchcock's *Psycho* style). HONESTLY, it's REALLY EFFECTIVE and much, much simpler than it appears to be. It's just really about communicating with yourself and discovering your unconscious parts and then checking how you are able to communicate with them.

What could be the ending of the "sweets conflict"? "Foodie" could be proposed to reduce the number of consumed goodies for other, healthier products that also give pleasure (e.g. favorite fruits with fresh yogurt and oats), while "health-conscious" could be proposed to allow shop-shelf sweets from time to time, while increasing the amount of physical exercise every day. Then, all you need is to propose a trial period and watch the results of the change.

The effects of coming to an agreement can be astounding: **the internal conflict disappears and—what's really important—the behavior transforms to become much more constructive and profitable.**

Try this process on any internal conflict you're experiencing and see what happens when you finally have come to a settlement between two parts!

Chapter 13: The Chain of Goals/Intentions

Here's how you can differently use the Chain of Goals technique mentioned in the previous chapter—not only to solve your internal conflicts, but also to work on many other things. It could be your procrastination, getting angry in certain situations, your laziness and stress recurring at specific times, or fear of meeting new people. It has to be something that is inside you, something about which you have an internal representation. Don't work on things and issues that are dependent on other people.

You can also pick something that is not a problem per-se, but needs to be improved. It could be motivation to do something, being more passionate about your project, waking up early, etc. The choice is yours.

Specify the thing you want to work on in one sentence as a concrete action or behavior (e.g. *"I'm always getting angry when...I always procrastinate when...I'm stressed out in situations like..."* etc.). Then take these steps:

1. Imagine a situation in which the problem or behavior specified by you takes place. Take a moment to relax and visualize this situation.
2. Think about a part of your body in which this piece of you being responsible for this action or behavior resides. Locate this spot.
3. Turn to this spot in your body where this part of yourself is and ask it, *"What do you want? What precisely do you want to achieve by doing that?"* Wait for the answer and then write it down on a piece of paper. This answer is your first intention. Say "thank you" to this part for giving you the answer.
4. Now, feel how it is when this new intention is entirely fulfilled, when you have fully obtained what this part of you wants to get by this initial behavior/action you're working on. Do as much as you can to feel it deeply and ask yourself this question, *"Once you have and fully feel (intention number 1 or further intentions) what you want to achieve by doing what you are usually doing,*

what's even more important now?" Wait for the answer and write it down. This is the next intention.

5. Create your chain of intentions this way, repeating step four, every single time feeling the further intention in the chain and asking yourself what's next. Do it until you can't answer the question from step four. It means that you have discovered the "original condition" or "core state": the ultimate, most important intention/goal you want to achieve.

For example, the whole process could look like this:

Problem: I'm totally stressed out before exams!

Question: What exactly do you want to achieve?

Answers: Prepare myself thoroughly. -> Intention 1: Pass the exams. -> Intention 2: Achieve the feeling of safety. -> Intention 3: Achieve the feeling of clearance. -> **Original intention:** Deep peace of mind.

The original intention is usually connected to a deep feeling of something, in a sense, a state of being: e.g. peace of mind, total calm, love, unity, presence, happiness. That's the state the part we are working with is following. It wants to achieve it by the action or behavior you want to change. It's really interesting as somehow this part of you came to a conclusion it will achieve that goal by acting or behaving like this..., but in a large majority of cases the outcomes are totally opposite. By discovering that, you can change it.

The last step of this exercise is getting into that original intention fully and deeply. Now, thinking about each of these intentions from your chain of goals, starting from the end, think how having the Original Intention (and still feeling it at the same time) changes or enriches having each of these intentions.

So, for example, having the instance above for consideration, you should first access the state of deep peace of mind (by physical exercise, visualizations or meditation, preferably using all three of these ideas), and then think about how having this peace of mind modifies or enhances the feeling of clearance. Give yourself a moment to feel and imagine it, then proceed to the next intention (feeling of safety). At the end, think about how having the Original State/Intention will influence the behavior or action you are working on. Try to fully feel every single intention, while being entirely in the Original Intention, and imagine for a moment how it changes every ring/step in your chain of goals. At the very end, pay attention to how your approach to the behavior or action you are working with has changed. You are probably looking at it differently now.

Remember, some kind of resistance may appear during the process. Your subconscious mind may protest at some point, for example, saying, *"But you can't be entirely happy!"* Then, see this objection as a part of yourself and ask it what precisely it wants to achieve by this protesting and start this exercise over again, this time with this new part. Once when you're done with it, go back to the place where you've previously stopped.

I'd like to note that this isn't a typical intellectual or logical process. **It's mainly about exploration and examination of your interior.** When answering the questions in this technique, listen to your intuition, not your logical mind. It's very important as we are working with your subconscious and what's sitting deep inside of you, not with your rational thinking.

Some people, on the other hand, are not sure if they are going to get any answers using this method. Don't worry about it—when you're turned towards your interior, you will get your answers quickly. Sometimes they will come to you as a premonition, sometimes it will be an image or symbol, sometimes a memory, internal dialogue or a sound. **Set yourself to listening and something will surely appear. Only then will you verbalize it and write it down on a sheet of paper.**

Regular practice of this technique will enable you to go through it quickly and easily. You can also print the steps of this technique and use them only when you feel you need them.

Chapter 14: How to Deal with the Past

Take a moment to reflect on your past. What do you see? Is it a source of strength and useful experiences for you, or rather a source of recurrent pain and suffering?

We often hear confessions like, *"These memories keep returning." "I regret what I did a few years ago." "How do I stop thinking about it?"* Luckily, there's an effective way of dealing with your past memories.

How old are you? Even if you're still young, you've surely been through a lot in your life already. Some moments were great, magnificent, worth remembering, whereas you would surely be eager to pay lots of money to have forgotten some of those less fortunate moments. **Which of these memories take up most of the space in your mind?**

There are people in this world who focus all their attention only on the unpleasant memories from their past. The more they want to forget about them, the bigger impact these thoughts have on them, and the more frequently they return. They experienced something unpleasant once and then they experience it again, again and again, ad infinitum, spending crazy amounts of time every day thinking about these past events and situations. They spend their entire lives thinking about the past.

It's exactly as if someone was driving a car looking in the rearview mirror all the time— not only is it impossible to reach the destination that way, but also it's extremely likely to cause some serious accidents. The rearview mirror is very useful, indeed, but only to take a look at it once in a while to find what's necessary at the moment. Still, you have to look at what's in front of you all the time. That's the only way to drive your car safely to your destination.

Remember what you were doing yesterday at this hour? This recalled memory will probably come together with a certain image. When did this image appear? Here and now. So, does the past exist anywhere else other than outside of your head? NO. **The past is nothing more than your imagination—a mind creation, collage of**

images, sounds and feelings. Just like a video recording. Is what you see on the recording real? Is it happening? No. It is only a reflection of reality. **Not reality itself.**

Let's state this again: the past does not exist. It is only a record in your head, in the form of multi-sensory memories. Why should you be worried so much about something that doesn't exist anymore? Why would you waste your life away focusing your attention on a videotape, on a stretch of reality which is recorded?

Think how many useless video recordings you still keep in your head that do nothing but hold you back. Put them aside, or you will go through all these negative emotions again and again, doing to yourself again what already ended a long time ago.

You can look at your past from many different perspectives. You can define it as a heavy burden you have to bear until the end of your life, or as very useful baggage of experiences, from which you will reap the wisdom just when you need it. Even the worst experiences can be viewed as a source of priceless teachings, which will provide you a helpful hand and direction sign on a desert in every difficult life situation.

When I sometimes work with people, I often come across those who regret what they have done in the past. I ask them, "Would you want to be in some other place in your life, different than you're in right now?" In the majority of the cases the answer is "*No.*" Then I tell them that every single element of their past life contributed to the fact that they now are where they are. It's like in the movie *The Butterfly Effect.* Appreciate every single experience from your past, because even the unpleasant ones can prove as a useful source of skills and knowledge to you.

I recently talked to a businessman, who told me a story of how once he lost huge amounts of money when his own co-worker robbed his office. He couldn't get over it for a long time and he couldn't let go of his anger and resentment. He really wanted his revenge, but finally, after some time, he decided to change his point of view to cease his suffering. He told me he now looks at this unfortunate situation as one of the most valuable lessons in his life. He's even grateful he got cheated, because now he pays more attention when picking new co-workers and cares much more about the safety of his business, thanks to which his new company grows much faster.

You can reframe every single memory like that. Everything is a matter of your perception. Looking from an entirely different perspective, you will feel totally different emotions. Always choose the perspective that is better for you. Change your view of certain situations and you will free yourself from excessive suffering.

Ask yourself these questions: Was what happened definitely a bad thing? Even if it was, what good can it bring into my life? What lesson have I learned? The answers will surely come and that's the moment when you start changing your detrimental perception of your past.

Mind you that liberating yourself from unpleasant memories doesn't mean erasing them from your life. They are, in a way, a part of who you are. You don't need to forget about where you came from, and how you became the person who you are now. **Your task is only to gain distance from what has happened,** so that you can free yourself from the negative impact of these memories. It's about you learning how to look at the past situation without thinking, *"Man, that was so horrible!"* Instead, think, *"What can I learn from that?"* Once you get rid of the negative impact, it will be much easier for you to reap reward from the experiences you gathered during all those years.

Once you have come to an understanding of that, you will suddenly realize that all people's chances are equal. Their past doesn't really matter that much. **It's not about where you came from, it's about where you're heading.** Where you grew up, what kind of childhood you had, what parents you had and which school you attended doesn't have to affect your future at all.

It is extremely important for you to know your past doesn't have to equal your future. The decisions about your future are always made here and now. Always make them taking your past experiences into consideration, but, before all, consider who you want to be in a month, one year, five years, etc. There's one NLP exercise I'm going to show you that will help you to finally deal with all of your negative memories. You will be able to start over again, leaving all your burden behind, and finally looking ahead with your chin up.

To begin, take a sheet of paper and start with writing down all the memories you can access in the form of keywords. Gather all the thoughts about your past that keep returning and inflicting bad emotions.

Then, pick one at a time and apply the NLP technique presented below. It is very important that you work on every single bad memory, once and for all liberating yourself from all these returning thoughts about your past.

Change of Personal History with NLP

1. Identify the memory you want to work on. If it's a situation you experienced more than once, pick the memory of the time when you experienced it for the first time. Close your eyes and imagine this situation as thoroughly as you can. Then, get into that memory as deeply as you can, feeling all these emotions that you then felt. Proceed to the next step once you're already immersed in that situation.
2. Now, break the state—do and think about something totally unrelated to that situation for a few minutes. Check your e-mail, cuddle your cat, count fruits in your kitchen or do anything else.
3. After five minutes, return to the technique and think what resource you'd need in that situation to make it a satisfactory experience instead of an unpleasant one— resource being an emotional state, skill or a certain belief. Maybe it could be the feeling of trust, being loved, self-confident or certainty that the other side had good intentions? Choose the resource that would entirely change your perception of that bad situation.
4. Focus on remembering if you had any situation in your life when you had this resource, fully and entirely? For example, when you really felt loved or self-assured? Pick certain memories that will bring you the desired emotional state. Close your eyes and bring back exactly what you then saw, felt and heard. Get into

that memory and recall all the emotions that were there. Once you are able to feel them fully, create the so-called "anchor" for the state—you need to establish a stimulus that will be connected to that particular feeling in your mind. I prefer kinesthetic anchors. You can, for example, touch the back of your hand with your fingers, grip your wrist a little bit or lightly pinch your ear. It should be unique, something you're not used to doing on a daily basis, such as scratching your nose.

5. Once you do this, break this state again. Then, close your eyes and go back to the negative memory, but this time see it as "dissociated", that is from the spectator's perspective (as a "third person"). Launch your anchor with the positive resource and watch yourself and the whole situation from aside. See how your entire behavior changes once you achieve the state you needed. See how the whole situation is changing along with the other people's behavior and your perception of that situation. Anchor that feeling.

6. Now go back to the beginning of that situation again and watch it again, this time "associated"—from your own eyes' perspective. Launch the positive anchor again and see how the situation is going once you've obtained the necessary resources. What is different in your perception of this situation? How's your behavior and other people's behavior changing? Give yourself the time to watch this situation until the end, then establish an anchor.

7. Check the effects. Bring back the feeling without launching the anchor and observe how the memory had changed. If you're still not satisfied with the change, go back to step 3 and go through the process again, this time choosing a different resource. If the negative emotions are gone—congrats!

Once you have worked through every single unpleasant memory, you're ready to take the next step. If you really want to bring back your memories, only go through the positive ones, the moments that give you joy and happiness.

The best solution is to move the majority of your thinking to the present and future. This kind of approach will give you more power and motivation and much more pleasure from living every day!

Chapter 15: How to Forgive

Anger and resentment aimed at other people are emotions which not only result in difficulties in building relationships with these people, these are the feelings which primarily destroy its host from within.

Sincere forgiveness requires great courage, but it's truly cleansing. Let me now show you a technique that will help you forgive and create inner peace.

Forgiveness is an art which you can use to escape the prison you have created for yourself by blaming others. Forgiveness will cleanse you from within and will allow you to regain the responsibility for the problems you couldn't deal with. Remember, it's not only about relieving others from their guilt—**the point being, you should do it to free yourself.**

Everything comes down to the very basics of NLP. **First of all, everyone has his own, individual model of this world.** Second of all, people make the best choices for themselves for a given moment, so their behaviors always have positive intents (not necessarily for you, but surely for them).

Have you ever experienced being totally misunderstood during a conversation, which later resulted in a conflict between you and that person? I experienced it a lot. Every single time I would wonder how it was possible the things that I said were perceived so negatively. So often, I would also feel very angry both at me and that person, which prevented me from solving the conflict.

You surely had to explain to other people, especially those important to you, that it wasn't what you meant, that you didn't have anything bad or offensive on your mind. You wanted to do well and you acted for a good reason. **So it was indeed—you had a positive intent,** but your message was misunderstood by the recipient. Maybe you wanted to help someone, but they thought you were questioning his competence. Maybe you wanted to comfort someone, but turned out you were not taking their problems seriously. Maybe you wanted to give someone a valuable feedback and they felt hurt by your words.

Whatever it was, misunderstanding of peoples' real intents leads to lot of bad consequences—arguments, unmet needs—all this makes it impossible to build a relationship based on trust and understanding.

Imagine a situation in which you are feeling deep, negative emotions connected to what someone said about you (or did to you). What's the reason for these emotions and did this person really have in mind exactly what you have received? Even if you think so, can you be perfectly sure?

The language we use to communicate with others limits what we can pass and communicate to others. In order to build a clear and possibly short message, we often omit lots of data that could often turn out to be crucial. Moreover, everyone sees reality differently and everyone understands certain words differently. Every single thing we communicate is exposed to being a big misunderstanding. You can NEVER be one hundred percent sure that you understood the intent of the person you are communicating with.

Now, look at it from a different way. Imagine yourself and some other person with whom you had and argument recently. Ask yourself, what positive intents could that person have? What could be the real meaning of the words that affected you so much?

Even when people do things considered as bad or evil, in their perception so often it is the best or the only possible solution for them. Even if you take an extreme example of violent parents who beat their children—you have to know they were probably beaten themselves as kids, never experienced love and care, and are now hardwired to believe that violence is the only effective tool to discipline and raise their kids. They are totally lost in their judgment, so often they think they are helping their children become reliable adults (which is their positive intent), and most usually they desperately need serious professional help. Now, am I justifying these cruel behaviors? Am I saying there's no such thing as objective guilt and, for example, murderers are innocent because they had positive intentions? Hell no! The bottom-line is, in everyday relations, in family relations or at work in business, we are so often blindfolded and don't want to understand that everyone acts according to their own set of rules and vision of reality. That's crucial. It's like in this Jane's Addiction song, "The Price I Pay:"

> *"I always do the wrong thing*
> *But for a very good reason*
> *Always do it wrong*
> *But it feels right"*

It's like in *Forrest Gump* – "shit happens" – to everyone, all of us, almost every single day. Yet, we rarely judge ourselves and the other people by exactly the same standards.

Notice that to even start considering forgiveness, you first have to recognize that someone is guilty for something. To consider someone guilty, you first need to have defined principles and frames related to the specific situation. The question is whether these principles are shared by the person you are trying to forgive? Is there anything to forgive at all, according to that person's perspective? Reflect for a moment if you're not playing a "judge", who assesses a person who behaved in a certain way according to his own personal guidelines.

So, can you expect people to always be perfect? Can you expect them to always be sure how to act in a given situation? Can you expect them to always place your own business in the first place and give it special priority? As human beings, we are conditioned to always care for our own good first—thanks to this, we have the biggest chance of survival.

However, people in relationships often act as if everyone around them only lives exclusively for them. When people lack self-esteem, they expect others to care about them —patting on the back, praising, helping and thinking about them all the time. When these expectations don't meet with reality, the "blame" suddenly appears, "He shouldn't have done that!" This conviction is the biggest mistake you can make. You have to know one thing—if somebody did it, they apparently needed it. Even if it was a mistake, maybe he needed this mistake to understand something important.

Forgiveness needs a deep understanding—you can't only look at the surface. **You have to reflect on the motives of a person and understand what drove that person.** Then, and only then, can you accept this conjuncture, putting your expectations aside. You can then understand that there's nothing to forgive as there is no guilt. So often, there's no real guilt, just an artificial creation of our mind, which believes in the dualistic concept of "good" and "bad".

Understanding the above is the first and very important step towards learning real forgiveness.

Now let me show you the second, equally important step—in the form of a specific process which will help you change your own approach.

Forgiveness 101

1. Choose a person whom you want to forgive. Think of the situation that is the subject of dispute.
2. First, think about yourself and ask, **"Has what happened in any way diminished who I am?"** Write the answer on a paper.
3. Now, think about the other person. What do you think drove him/her? What were his/her motives and beliefs? **What was his/her goal?** Determine his/her **positive** intention and write the answer on a paper.
4. What exactly was the person lacking in that specific situation which kept him/her from acting differently? What resources, emotions or beliefs they lacked? Could it be lack of safety? Of understanding and trust? Maybe they lacked the belief they could do well on their own? Write down the **lacking resources** on a paper.
5. Imagine the person in that specific situation. Think about the positive intention. Now hand him/her the lacking resources and see how his/her behavior changes once they obtain them. See how the situation goes and ends.
6. Now, imagine you appear there, in that situation, with the opportunity to look in the person's eyes and forgive him/her. Smile, hug him/her and say, **"I forgive**

you with my whole heart. I also forgive myself that I poisoned myself with anger and resentment. Thank you!"

7. Open your eyes and see the results—think about that person and about the situation and see how you feel.

If you want to forgive anyone, test the above process right now. Let your relationship be full of warmth and understanding—learn how to truly forgive, and you will get ready for the next step, which is **understanding, where you decline the concept of blame, and then, by assumption, you will always forgive everyone.**

Chapter 16: Leave It Behind

If you want beautiful flowers to flourish in your garden, you need to get rid of weeds first. Sometimes, you need to leave something behind to free some space for new things. Our egos tend to tie to people, things and places, so this process is not always simple. We are often stuck in one place, afraid of letting things go. Yesterday, when I was travelling on a train, observing how everything disappears on the line of horizon, I came across an interesting idea for a simple exercise involving a little bit of imagination that might help you get rid of the emotions stuck to you, even when you are ready to let them go once and for all.

If you're not over your emotional bond to a certain thing or a person you want to let go, strenuous attempts to forget may not bring in any results. The emotions will keep coming back.

The process of setting yourself free demands your attention. Instead of trying to escape from the returning thoughts, invite them over. Concentrate on what keeps coming back to finally release the emotions, images and internal dialogues reminding you about the things you want to forget so much.

For instance, let's say you want to get rid of the returning thoughts about your ex-girlfriend/boyfriend. Let's assume you wanted to be together, but for some reason that was not to be.

First of all, it is very important to ask yourself, *"What was this relationship giving me? What needs were fulfilled? What exactly do I miss and lack now? Proximity, partnership, a sense of security? What is another way by which I can obtain these things?"* Answers to these questions will help you realize that usually there are many other ways to fill your life with what's important to you. Sometimes that's not enough—your mind might already have a habit of constantly focusing your thoughts on that person, especially if that was someone you loved.

In that situation, you need to focus on the process, especially on certain thought patterns showing up in your head most frequently. You can do this using many of the techniques from this book, but sometimes, if the trauma and memories are really strong and deeply rooted, you might need to take a few sessions with a certified psychotherapist.

Anyway, here's my idea for a helpful exercise. You can apply this technique if you want to leave something behind and you are ready to free yourself from the burden of destructive emotions that keep coming back to you. It is a very simple process that will effectively influence your subconscious, sending your mind the information, *"Now I can leave it behind."*

Since I'm a devoted old-school Nokia phones fan (those indestructible phones with keyboards and no internet connection, I don't use smartphones at all—can you believe it?), I didn't really have a camera decent enough to record the view from the back car myself, but I have found this very nice video recorded by someone else on YouTube instead: tinyurl.com/backcar

Before you launch it, think about that thing you want to leave behind. It could be recurring thoughts about a person that has disappeared from your life, emotions connected with the loss of a material good, or an urge to return to the place you used to live in before you moved.

In your imagination, put a symbol of this thing on railroad tracks (if it's a person, then tell them to quickly leave the tracks after you are done with the exercise : -)) and start the video on full screen.

Observe as the thing slowly fades away until its disappearance on the horizon. See how you feel and repeat the process, if necessary.

The process won't always be pleasant—you might feel empty inside after you are done. It's perfectly normal and it's important for you to fill this emptiness with something else. Once again, ask yourself the question I wrote about in this chapter and find new ways to fulfill the needs important to you.

Chapter 17: Perceptual Positions

Have you ever argued with a loved one while being so entirely focused on your own point of view, you never really noticed what the person was trying to tell you?

The majority of conflicts come from lack of ability to incarnate in the role of another person and see things from his/her perspective. People are often attached to the only one limited way of viewing reality, which brings lots of interpersonal conflicts.

It's time to change your perspective.

The concept of perceptual positions was started by Virginia Satir, a family therapist. She urged their patients to look at their own problems from the perspective of other family members. It turned out that many times the change in point of view opened access to entirely fresh information about conflicts or problems in their life. Moreover, so often the conflict would then disappear and family members would apologize to each other for their egoistic behaviors.

A look from a different perspective alone gives you access to entirely different, new resources. When being held a prisoner by only your own point of view, you lose lots of extremely important info and feedback, and you are ready to fight for your own point never realizing that the other person might in fact be right about something.

Joseph O'Connor wrote:

Observation from a single point of view is carried out in one narrow perspective that is real when you look at the problem from a certain angle, but doesn't give the holistic view. We only see a stretch of reality when we need both the awareness of detail, zoom and insight into the full depth of an issue.

Looking at things only from one perspective is like looking at the world exclusively through your window. When you remain in your room all the time, you will always see the same strip of reality. Nonetheless, **make a "trip" to another room and you will see a totally different world in the window.**

Three Points of View

NLP distinguishes three basic perceptual positions. The ability to move between them will give you great flexibility and access to completely new opportunities. You will be able to handle conflicts better (given there will be any), think far more creatively, learn from your past mistakes more effectively and also learn new things much faster.

The first perceptual position is a view from the perspective of "me"—your own convenient perspective. From this place, you are able to notice what is important to you personally. When you recall past situations in your own life, in this perceptual position you see them in "association", which means they are seen from the perspective of your own eyes. You follow your own needs, observe the world through the prism of your own beliefs and experiences.

The second perceptual position is another person's point of view. It's about "incarnation" into someone else's skin and looking into the situation/issue from their perspective. You reflect on how that person might feel, what was important to that person in a given situation and what could that person need. What beliefs would that person have? **Imagine you are that person; experience the situation as if you were that person.** The ability to enter into this perceptual position will allow you to really know what empathy is. You will be surprised how differently the world looks from that perspective. If, for example, you argued with that person and their points appeared strange and irrational, you will be able to see they were perfectly normal and their behavior was understandable from their perspective. You will get to know this person's world map, which is crucial to building healthy and meaningful relationships.

The third perceptual position is the observer's perspective. It's about being someone entirely independent, someone who is not affiliated in any way with the situation. That means going beyond both yours and the other involved person's perspective. It is a key to noticing the relationship between actions of the two sides of the conflict, the similar patterns of thoughts and behaviors. In this perspective, you are able to get rid of any emotional impact and able to notice more. When, for instance, you're looking at the conflict between you and another person, pick a place aside and imagine you are observing you and the other person from there. Carefully listen to what you are saying to each other and the relationship between you. Be an independent observer, spectator and just a point in the space that has nothing in common with the conflict.

I want you to know that every single one of these positions is very significant. **None is more important than the others.** What's very crucial here is the ability to move between these positions. You surely know some people that are always looking at the world only from their own perspective. They usually act extremely selfishly, never paying any attention to other people's needs. However, people who look from the second perspective too often are very vulnerable to other people's impact, thinking about what others might think all the time. People who spend most of their time in the third position usually look "detached" and "distant", like they don't have any feelings at all. That's why it's so important to find a balance here and to pick your point of view depending on the situation, experiencing how it looks from each single position.

<u>By being aware of the existence of perception positions and possibly getting into them, you gain a big advantage and a very efficient mind tool.</u>

There are two more perceptual positions—looking from the perspective of the system (paying attention to the relations between single elements) and from the perspective of the universe (how your actions impact the whole world) —but they're a topic for a whole other book. I now want you to focus on these three, as they will bring you the most noticeable change.

There are many uses of this concept. Here are some examples and ideas for you to try:

1. **Conflicts and arguments.** Here's where the perceptual position proves the most helpful and useful. Getting into the other person's perspective and then seeing the whole thing through the eyes of an independent observer, you will

quickly understand where the conflict comes from and so you will be able to resolve it sooner. When I use the second position, I often think to myself, *"How could I have my eyes fixed on my point so stubbornly? I wasn't even right at all!"* Perceptual positions are also very useful in negotiations.

2. **Creative problem solving.** Ask yourself the question, *"How would my friend/girlfriend/wife/children/parents/coach/president of the country/Santa Claus/whoever is important in this case look at it?"* Reflecting on these points of view you will be able to find entirely new ideas. This applies to all sorts of life problems, and also moments when you want to come up with creative solutions while working on a project.

3. **Business creation.** Take your clients' perspective. Think what they might think, what might they want, what kind of problems they deal with? For instance, when you want to open a restaurant, visit one as a client first, constantly observing how you act as a client, what do you expect from the place you are visiting. Write down all your conclusions. Then take observer's perspective and see how the process of sale looks from here. What are the relations between the seller and the client?

4. **Dealing with past experiences.** If you have past memories that keep returning and haunting you, affecting you negatively, like in the example from the previous chapter, "How to Deal with the Past," return to them in your imagination and see them from many different perspectives. You will eventually notice that you are the one to give these situations so much significance and that they often don't look that bad from a different point of view.

5. **Learning new behaviors.** Do you want to be more self-confident? Remember a situation when you didn't have the resource of self-confidence and look at it from different perspectives. Observe what you were missing and how you should react so that people start seeing you differently. Then imagine the same situation in the future, when you want to act confidently. Look from many different perspectives, also from your own, when you're using the resource of self-confidence.

6. **Public appearances.** When I'm about to give a public speech, I often sit on different chairs in the audience and observe the spot where I'm going to speak. I get into the role of someone who will have to listen to me for a while and notice

many new things that I wouldn't know otherwise. This way I'm able to prepare myself much better for the speech.

7. **Self-development.** Look at yourself from other people's perspective. Look at who you are, where are you going, what kind of person you are in the relationships. Write down your insights, you will see that there will be plenty—some of them will be astonishing and maybe you would otherwise come across them a few years later, if at all. Then look at yourself as an independent spectator and observe your behaviors and actions.

There are many other applications of these three perceptual positions, and you will surely discover them yourself. It's a great tool and a habit/ability that is worth having. Since I started using this technique, I'm able to notice much more things in my life, **which in turn allows me to improve faster.**

Different Perspectives in Practice

I will now show you the practical exercise that will help you begin to start with the concept you just read about. **Once you learn how to move between these three perspectives, you will be able to do it almost automatically, just by closing your eyes.** The truth is, you could even do it now. If you want, you can use this exercise from the beginning—it will surely help you experience more deeply what the perceptual positions are.

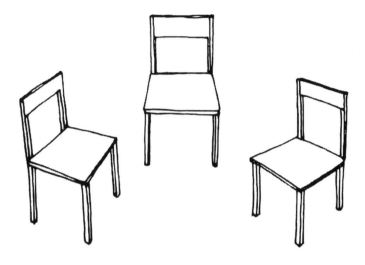

Set three chairs in a circle, like shown above in this artistically resplendent drawing of mine. On each chair, you can put cards "me", "the other person" and "observer" written on them, but it's not necessary.

Now, identify a situation to which you want to apply the perceptual positions. It can be some kind of argument, business negotiation, interview or an ordinary conversation with your friend. Pick a situation you want to change or have a better insight and learn from. Now, beginning from the first perceptual position, sit on each chair and assume the different point of view every single time. Close your eyes on each chair and imagine the situation. **Remember to have a pen with you—you should write down your insights.** Pay attention to your body language, to words you are using, the course of the whole situation, and to other people's behavior.

Arrangement of these seats in space is very important since, in a way, it gives your mind an implication that these are three different points of view. **You will see that the change of seat alone will give you a different perspective.** It's a technique successfully used by many successful psychotherapists all around the world. There can be more chairs, if there's more people involved in this situation. You can use this exercise either to think over situations that already happened or events yet to come.

NLP is about enriching your experience so you gain a wider perspective and better access to your resources. Perceptual positions can become a part of your world view that will surely help your self-development and make your life simply better.

"Man's mind, once stretched by an idea, never regains its original shape."

- Oliver Wendell Holmes

Chapter 18: Make Others Feel Good Around You

This is an absolute foundation of human relations. If you want to attract other people and make them comfortable and happy around you, I am going to show you this simple concept, which will help you look differently at your role in creating strong human relationships.

Have you ever wondered how it was possible that some people acted like big human attractors and what did they do or had inside of them that made everyone else want to be around them? How does it work—everyone wants to hang out, talk and have fun with them, whereas you don't experience that too often?

The first thing you have to understand is the fact that they don't own anything you don't have. The difference lies in what **they do that you probably don't do.** (I wrote "probably" because there's a possibility some readers don't feel the urge to improve that area of their life. I thought the same until I found out about this concept though.) The difference is in doing or not doing certain things, not about having certain traits. It's not about telling compliments to other people.

Another very important thing to remember—**the relationship with another human being always starts from you.** What does that mean? Before you even meet the person and start talking and connecting, you already have an impact on how this conversation will look. I'm referring to the feelings and emotions you have inside of you before you start creating a new relationship. Remember, every contact with another person is a creation of some kind of relationship. **Here it is: your emotional state is the most important thing,** when it comes to making people feel comfortable around you and making them want to build relations with you. If you feel bad, miserable and nervous, and just then you meet someone and start the conversation, this person will most probably also start feeling bad very soon. If someone feels bad around you, they don't want to meet you too often... if at all.

When you feel great, are smiling and joyful, other people will feel the same when you're around them. You will be vibrating with positive energy and they will feel it. **These vibrations will affect them and make them feel good and joyful in your company** (the spiritual-sounding "vibrations" are just the effect of the so-called "mirror neurons" doing their job). That's the most important reason for which people will love to be around you more frequently.

Every single time when you're about to interact with anybody, do everything to make yourself feel good first. Do something to smile and feel great (do what it takes—have your favorite dish, dance, exercise or watch an episode of your favorite comedy series), then meet people. Your emotional state will radiate on everyone you're with. People around you will feel better and will want to spend more time with you. It's very easy and effective, but yet so few people know it.

As an exercise, I want you to apply this for the next few days. Effects are immediate, and the knowledge that people around you feel good because of your attitude is really precious and inspiring. You will get a chance to gain new friends who will love to spend time around you.

Let's now do some practical exercises!

1. Let's do some acting. Go back to the chart from the chapter "How to Release Destructive Emotions" (or just click <u>HERE</u>) that shows different emotions. Pick some of the negative emotions you have felt most frequently in the last week.

   Stand in front of a mirror and act like you're feeling the emotions, or much better —do what you can to get into them again. Imagine all these situations that brought you these negative emotions. Now, watch your face in the mirror. How does your face and body language look? Do you like how you look then? Do you want others to see you and remember you like that? If you stick to this exercise, and do it a few times, you will possibly remember how bad you look when you're going through bad emotions. Any time you feel these emotions again, you will remember your face in the mirror and will have better motivation to get rid of them (or simply refrain from feeling them, sometimes it really is just that easy).

2. Do the same things, but with all these positive emotions you felt lately. Do you like your look now? Do you like it more when you look vibrant and happy? Don't you think people around you would feel much better seeing you that way? Would you like to be remembered that way and described that way by word of mouth? Try to oppose how you look when you feel good to how you look when you feel bad. Try to create a strong contrast in your head between these two opposite images.

3. This exercise is a little bit similar to the previous ones. This time, though, you don't need a mirror. Try to enter different emotions, and being in them, say different sentences aloud (the ones you would normally feel going through these emotions). Hear the difference in your voice, its sound, pitch, speed of talking etc.

Now, you always hear your voice a little bit differently than others. Reflect on that. Is it possible that sometimes you are acting grumpy because of the tone of your voice (and possibly also different parameters), without even knowing it?

Chapter 19: Always Start from Yourself

During your entire life, you have created and will be creating relationships with other people. No matter if they are male-female relations, long friendships, new connections or anything else, you've probably worked all the time to make the relationships better.

Were you having the outcomes you wanted?

When building relationships, most of people are afraid of taking responsibility for how they really work. When things go awry, they shift the responsibility to their surroundings and wash their hands of it, like biblical Pilate. In the majority of cases, it's their partner's fault, because how could it be any other way? They don't understand, they are not interested and—honestly—they just think about themselves and only perceive the world looking from their own perspective. Then, deciding for the "only possible method" of relationship maintenance, they decide to...repair their partner.

Because *"He/she HAS to change!"*

Because *"If he/she isn't fulfilling my expectations, he/she has to start doing something about it!"*

In their perspective, it's the only possibility of healing the relationship. I know this from my own experience—I did that as well. Fortunately, the time came when I realized how limited and unwise this type of thinking really is.

Being in a relationship (not necessarily a romantic one, it also applies to friendships and other types of relations), maybe you have created a certain vision of your partner that fits you the most. You've created a perfect image of that person, how he/she SHOULD be. When later this vision didn't coincide with the reality of who the person really was, you started experiencing the suffering, explaining with many rationalizations, such as, *"He/she doesn't care about my needs," "He/she just thinks about him/herself,"* etc.

But who's really making a mistake here? The person that doesn't meet the expectations or the person who created them in the first place? Remember, the more idealized version of your partner you create in your mind, the more difficult it will be for you to enjoy the relationship. Leave your irrational expectations towards the people around you. <u>Stop living in relationships with the "perfect" mental hallucinations. Start seeing the people for who they REALLY are.</u>

Let me try to explain the dynamics of some relations to you more clearly. Let's say that the relationship you are in isn't developing and flourishing as you'd like it to, so you tell to your partner, "Listen, we both see that something isn't really working in our relationship. Of course, I am perfectly fine and there's nothing I can be blamed for. Looks like something's bad with you. It happens that I know what and I can expand on that. Let me do it and then when I'm done I will tell you exactly what to do to change yourself. I will modify you so that you finally go along with my expectations. Because, you know, I have created a vision of perfect you and now I'm on my mission to make you fit in it. So, do we have a deal? Just so you know, as soon as you change as I wanted you to, we'll be talking differently. I will start threatening you with a breakup and everything will end. So move! I will be here waiting patiently, let me know once you have changed."

Sounds ridiculous... or maybe familiar? It looks exactly like that in so many relationships. Of course no one is saying these words exactly, but this is just what some people have on their minds. By this exaggeration here I wanted to make you realize one very important thing: so often we want our partners to change, being sure they are the ones generating the problem, while in reality it's all the other way around. We create a perfect vision of a person and then we have a problem that something doesn't fit in. Wake up!

If you want your relationship to be better, healthier and happier—ALWAYS BEGIN FROM YOURSELF. ALWAYS! It is one of the most important things I've learned in the context of building happy relationships.

At the beginning, there might be some inner resistance appearing. *"What? Why should I change? I am okay!"* Maybe you are okay indeed. At the same time, you have to realize that any effort to change your partner will result in a failure anyway, sooner or later. You will just make the situation worse and worse, making your partner miserable at the same time. Anyway, would you like to see your partner working on the plan of inventing you over so that you become more similar to his/her own version of the "perfect" you?

Allow your partners to be themselves, and you will give them the best gift in the world. And if you want to live with them better and happier—that's great! Work on your beliefs, behaviors, emotions and expectations. I guarantee you that you will discover lots of things that restrain you from creating meaningful and deep relationships. I still do, even though I really believed I was developed enough in the matter of relationships.

Stop looking for an external salvation. Every single relationship is INSIDE of you. Your partner is a mirror in which you see yourself. **Every single time you feel negative emotions towards your partner, in reality you learn something about yourself.** When you dedicate yourself to making your relationship better and decide to work on yourself first, these two situations might occur:

The first possibility is that you will change for the better and your partner will not. What's the outcome? Better relationship. You will be a better partner, you will be better at understanding that person, you will be a better communicator. Worse comes to worst, you will break up like you would without doing anything to solve the problem, only in this case you will end this relationship as a better, developed person, and it will be much easier for you to find another one, or be perfectly happy single. Nonetheless, the first option has a very low probability. It's far more probable that the second option will occur. The second option comes down to your partner seeing your transformation and following you. What's the effect of this most likely version? A much better, stronger and constantly developing relationship.

When you stop being offended by everything, you partner will stop as well. If you stop complaining, he/she will probably also stop at some point. If you start listening carefully, you will be listened to more often (mirror neurons!) ... **Be the one to start the process of change and development. Become a living example for your partner.**

This approach is very efficient and healthy when it comes to building relationships based on firm and durable foundations. Start from yourself and don't look anywhere else for confirmation and approval. Don't look if your partner has already started changing or not. Get rid of your expectations and start working on yourself. Before anything, do it for yourself as you will feel much better doing so. This is the most consistent approach, thanks to which your relationship will start developing truly and quickly. Your partner will notice it sooner or later, but it shouldn't matter to you. You are not doing it for that person to change. You are doing it because you want to live on better terms with that person, have a better relationship and be happier.

Go ahead and test it yourself. You will be surprised how fast the effects will come. When I first discovered all this I just wrote about, my relationships with others changed massively. I'm really glad I freed myself from the constant need of changing the people I live with. It means freedom, both for me and for them. Now, it's your turn. At the earliest occasion, think about this chapter. Start noticing all these things you haven't been noticing in your relationship so far, as from now on it will just start getting better and better.

On that note, when we are talking about "changing other people", let me expand on something else. Let's say you want someone to change because you think you feel sorry for them or you feel pity for them. Here's the truth—**pity and compassion are, in fact, harmful emotional states.** Yes, I just said that. Any time I state that, people think I'm some kind of psychopath, but let me now desecrate this myth of usefulness of mercy through the pity and compassion which is so popular in our culture, so that you can understand what I have on my mind.

When we are talking about "compassion", the word itself means you are compassionate and sympathetic with the person's feelings (or, more precisely, you think you are, and you think that you can feel exactly the same thing). To put it in different words—you are uniting in, for example, despair. You feel exactly the same thing (or again, you think so); in fact, one of you just nods emotionally and mimics the other person, thereby becoming unnecessary and useless in this situation. It's like in this mindless saying that a successful relationship consists of two halves, which suggests that one person is a buttock and the other one is a half-bum, too. Successful relationships don't consist of two halves, but of two whole persons. I'm not a half and neither is my woman! Thanks to that, we can harmoniously create a bigger whole.

Compassion means you are becoming a sheep—you join the herd and start acting the same, singing the same pointless song. There's also mercy. *"To lean over someone with mercy"*—for me, pity and mercy indicate a sense of superiority and the recognition of other people as hopeless victims, unable to rise on their own feet, take independent action and fight over something or for something. There's some kind of sadistic power and haughtiness in mercy and pity, at least I feel so. Empathy, though, is different.

What's the difference between pity and empathy? The compassionate one feels compassion, whereas empathy means **understanding**. NOT emotional solidarity/unity. You're truly emphatic when you understand what someone is going through, maybe because you've "been there and done that," maybe because you have once recovered from similar or even a bigger crisis or problem and you know you can offer a firm, helpful hand. You **don't** help others by turning yourself into useless, trembling emotional jelly, saying that you *"feel the same"* (honestly, you most probably don't, and if you do, that's even worse), but by motivating and inspiring someone towards taking the right action.

Empathy, in a practical context, means you understand what someone struggles with, so you can help. You can, because you understand. Emotions are overrated in this particular context. Mutual crying won't solve a single thing. Mutual laughter, neither. Only effective action solves problems.

I always liked the metaphor of sheep and the shepherd dog. The dog is rather snippy when interacting with the herd, spurs them, barks at them and doesn't treat them too gently. At the same time, the dog is the herd's protector from their worst enemies: wolves. The shepherd dog doesn't give a crap what the sheep think of him (let's now look at the dog as a human being, for the sake of this metaphor), not because he's indifferent or mean, but because he's loyal to the task he has to accomplish. He's on the duty of protecting the herd. He has to defend them, not be liked. He's there to **really** help—not to be accepted

117

in order to feel good (*"Hey, look! Over here! I'm a nice and righteous guy!"*). He's harsh, but that's his mission. He's entirely focused on it.

That's exactly why empathy is good, where compassion and pity are often (not ALWAYS, in EVERY single instance, but VERY often) detrimental.

That's the attitude you want to have when someone needs you and wants you to help them. If you can and want to help someone, you have to be strong enough to do that and come from a strong frame, instead of acting like you were hurting or experiencing a big problem yourself. You are not drowning in the sea, but standing on a boat from where you can drop a rope, so don't act like you're drowning, too. That wouldn't be too helpful for someone who is struggling to stay afloat in cold and stormy waters.

At the end, mind you that this chapter was about rather healthy and "normal" relationships between two mature people. That being said, I don't think you should blame yourself for crazy actions and behaviors of toxic people, also known as "emotional vampires" and try to improve/repair something that never really worked in the first place. Just do everything not to have anything in common with these people. They will only drain you, squeeze you and leave you miserable. That might include dating people with drug/alcohol problems, emotionally unstable and self-destructive, sticking to people in debt who you don't know that much and who just use you as a portable ATM, "friends" who never respect your time, people who do nothing but criticize and judge everyone and everything, people involved in organized crime, etc. You are NOT obligated to help them and the truth is you can't help them (they will do everything to make you believe so—that's what we call "manipulation" and "gaming" people). However rough it might sound, the only people who can help them are themselves. You can't change anyone without their permission, and you don't have any obligation to do so. You don't want to be around these people. Never start any relationships with them in the first place, and if you already have —quit ASAP and never look back! This is a broad and really deep topic for a whole other book, but I just felt that it was an important thing to mention, not to leave you confused on that matter.

Chapter 20: How to Free Yourself from Other People's Opinions and Judgments

Sharp words and negative opinions are the biggest source of suffering for some people. Giving other people the permission to be emotionally manipulated with words, they are really the creators of their own suffering. Maybe you are one of these people who allow others to influence their emotions this way. It's high time for you to get liberated. How do we feel what we want, no matter what the others say?

Once, when I was a kid, I had this elementary school friend, Mike. He was a funny, cheerful, easy-going and creative boy—he was really skilled with tools and wood stuff, such as carpentry. He was probably born with a saw and hammer in his hands. He could have been a great furniture maker. He was able to literally carve art out of wood when he was eight. Also, every time Mike told a joke or made an impression of someone (usually a teacher or a celebrity), everybody would instantly roll on the floor laughing. Girls thought he was cool (but he didn't know that and wouldn't believe that, no matter how long we convinced him). He was also very skilled at sports, especially extreme-ish BMX bike riding. Unfortunately, he was not really the best math and languages student. He always got confused with numbers (just like I did), could never remember his history lessons and his German sucked (he probably just never knew HOW to learn). I really liked to spend my time with him. We would run all around the forests with wooden swords, build tree houses on all our free days and have loads of fun.

Sadly, his mother was not an emotionally intelligent person. Every time Mike brought bad grades home, she would get furious. She used to spend hours screaming at him, throwing names and, sometimes, throwing things. Once I witnessed that she threw a tennis ball right in his face, from as close as three feet, using her full power. I was horrified—he wasn't hurt, but it surely was humiliating. She often told him he would never amount to anything, that he was a total moron, and that if he kept getting bad grades, he would eventually become an unemployed alcoholic and start living under the bridge.

Unfortunately, **he believed it**. He really did. He was just a little kid. A self-fulfilling prophecy had started to come true. His father tried to support him and defend him, but he was a "beta", submissive, weak "nice guy" type, without much willpower and they were all under the strong influence of that woman. Mike was getting worse and worse. Teachers wouldn't help, as he had lost his motivation to learn and kept getting bad grades. We really tried to cheer him up and help him, but his mother's strong, dark influence reigned over him and messed with his inexperienced mind more and more. At that point, he would often talk about creepy stuff, such as how bad life was, how cruel people were and how he would like that plane flying above us to fall down and crash, so he could see all the rich people die in a fire. We were really terrified to listen to those sort of ghastly things (by the way, his family wasn't poor, they were regular suburbs people). We were just nine- or ten-year-old little boys. We played violent video games sometimes, but some of us still slept with our teddybears. We slowly started looking for some other friends. Kids want to have fun. At some point, when we graduated from elementary school, his mum forbade us from seeing him because she believed he should sit home and learn all the time.

Then, he started having drug and alcohol problems at the young age of sixteen. His self-confidence declined significantly even more during the next few years. Then his mother "woke up" and realized she had wrecked her son's confidence and annihilated his ability to learn anything new, but it was already way too late. She probably wanted him to become a good and educated person, but she failed to understand he would never be a good lawyer or doctor (that's, of course, who she wanted him to be). He would surely make a great stand up-comedian, or a carpenter. Ironically, his dad was one—a great one—and he was making more money with his services and handmade furniture than my dad earned as a history professor at that time. That's what I could never understand about that woman and that whole family—talk about the destructive power of social conditioning. He could have been anyone he wanted, if she was more forbearing.

At some point, I moved to another city to start learning at a good university. Mike stayed in our little western hometown, started seeing some really bad people and got stuck in a big drug problem. Then, I moved to another country, across the ocean. I knew from our mutual friend that he had his ups and downs, but generally, his life was very low all the time. He would either drink or take drugs or play computer games at home, still living with his toxic mum, who now realized what she really did and tried everything to help him, mainly forcing him to go to AA/drug meetings, asking his ex-friends to do something about him (how ironic) and trying to send him to different courses or any college. At that point, no one could really get to him and pierce through the hard shell he had grown on himself during all these years. Then, he probably changed phone numbers or something happened and we totally lost contact. It was just a few years ago I found out about him from our mutual friend. He stopped drinking and went to college to another city, but still he uses drugs sometimes. He just started college (he should've already finished it a few years ago), and because of his wrecked self-confidence, he has NEVER had a girlfriend. That is how he is doing now. A good looking guy with HUGE potential.

It still haunts me until today. I wish I could have helped him, but none of us could at that point. We all failed big time. He truly BELIEVED what his mother kept telling him—he was worthless, stupid, slow, awkward and hopeless and what not.

I know this is really a sad story. Why I am telling you this? (By the way, what are you feeling right now? Where does it comes from and what could it mean?) I am doing it to make you realize **HOW MUCH** you can hurt a person with words (especially an innocent kid!), when they believe in what you say about them. Or, for the sake of this chapter, how much you can get hurt by others when you **let them.**

Maybe someone offended you by saying you play baseball like a five-year-old, or maybe that you didn't have any sense of humor or could not sing. Whatever it was, it could influence your life and emotions in many different ways, especially if you were young. The most important thing to realize here is the fact that any given opinion can impact you only when... you believe it.

Every single time the reason you felt all these negative emotions after you've been told something mean was because **you believed it**, more or less. Otherwise, any opinion or intended offense couldn't trigger these bad emotions in you. The fact that you've believed in all these negative things about you means your beliefs about yourself weren't strong enough. **You gave your own authority away to them, which made you believe all those people instead of trusting yourself.**

When you're a grown-up or teenager, the fact that you believe in other people's opinion about yourself is **nothing but your own problem**—definitely not theirs. You can cry and scream as loud as you like, "They offended me!" In reality, **it is you offending yourself.** The one who judged you negatively has probably just done it once or a few times, **but you could be the one to repeat it in your mind hundreds of times**, worsening your emotional state with every single repeat. If someone tells you, "You're uncultured and vulgar!" and you feel bad, it means you really think so about yourself. You allow the possibility of that statement being true to your consciousness. **That's the only reason for your negative emotions, not the fact that some other person said so.**

Take responsibility for your own emotions, as you are the one causing them. Every single emotion you experience is an effect of the thoughts you think every single day. Depending on what beliefs you have about yourself and what images of your future you create, so you will feel. You will be a slave to other people's opinions and words, unless you decide to take action. You will be a believer in a big fiction—that other people can affect and influence your emotions.

Why would you get angry and suffer when someone tells you their opinion that hurts your ego? These emotions will seriously damage your ability to act intelligently in these situations. It can even lead you to actions you will eventually regret. You need calmness and self-control to act effectively and consciously make the best decisions.

The responsibility is yours to take as NO ONE can affect your emotions without your concession. Again, it really can't be said enough—if you think someone has hurt you with their words, it's only because you had allowed it. **Comprehension of the fact is the first and the biggest step to emotional freedom.**

Let alone the fact that roughly 96% of what people say isn't even their own opinion. If someone directs unpleasant words at you, it's much more probable they just want to make you feel bad (either consciously or sub-consciously), because they feel bad themselves. If you let them, you give them clear permission to manipulate you. Words are just tools. In the case of negative feedback, they usually don't go along with that person's opinions, but are a result of the person's emotional state. Take a look in the past and think how many times have you heard *"I didn't really mean that!"* from someone you love?

Wouldn't that be really idiotic to believe in words of a person that never believed they were true in the first place? Still, the vast majority of this planet's inhabitants are torturing themselves, believing in false opinions that were brought up just to make them feel bad. As soon as you come to this realization, you gain real freedom. You begin noticing how it really works and can wisely decide what to believe and what not to believe. Other people's words can only hurt when you give them meaning. But before the emotional reaction comes, there's a gap in which you can decide how to feel.

If you get hurt by anyone's words ever again, that will be a very important moment to you —it's when you will discover your weak point. **It will mean you still have strings attached to yourself, which other people can pull, making you act like a puppet.**

Although earlier you might think about people that have negative opinion about you as your enemies, now they will become your best teachers. Every time they hurt you with their words, you will learn a lot about yourself. **You will find the weak spot on which you should work.** By the next time you will be stronger and the opinion won't affect you that much, if at all.

Your goal is to reach the state where no matter if someone says something mean about you, your life or the person that is important to you, you will still be able to choose to feel as great as before these words had been said. **It's called emotional freedom, when you're the one to decide how you want to think, feel and act.** Who knows, maybe you're free right now, when you're reading this book. Sometimes, it's all about a little single incentive that makes you take a big leap on the path of your development. We have talked a lot about believing and not believing. Let me now tell you about how you can change your beliefs about anything.

Chapter 21: Change of Beliefs

Change of beliefs can be seen as a chore for some people. To leave behind a current belief and adapt a new one surely requires an open mind. You should know that change of beliefs is one of the most efficient ways of changing your behaviors.

Think about it—is it easy to start a business when someone believes, *"All people are deceitful and just want to take advantage of others, and money is bad because it spoils people"*? Will this person get results? Now, think about a person that believes everyone is special and money is really useful and can be used to massively help others and make the world better? See the difference?

Exercise time! Take a sheet of paper and write down every single belief limiting you. Everyone has lots of beliefs to change, so calmly and thoroughly reflect on what beliefs hold you back and keep you away from achieving your goals. For example: *"This world is a gloomy place." "It's difficult to make money." "I'm a loser." "I don't know how to talk with people." "Learning languages is difficult,"* and so on. I could give you countless examples—people who stick to these beliefs just hurt themselves big time. You don't want to remain one of them!

So, cross out all these negative beliefs you have written down and list their opposites. Remember, the new beliefs should be formulated positively (e.g.: *"I'm really handsome"* instead of *"I don't look that bad"*). As soon as you have your list of positive beliefs, you can start working on them.

For the change to occur, these two conditions have to be met:

First of all, you need to want to change. So always ask yourself if you want to entirely and truly change your belief, and whether you are congruent with this decision. Think what consequences faith in a certain belief brings you and if you could have any subconscious benefits from staying faithful to that belief. If not—that's great—the first condition is met.

Second of all, you have to give yourself a chance to change, meaning you have to believe the transformation is possible. If you believe so, then you will give yourself a chance and try this exercise. Open your mind as you have nothing to lose here. I've changed my detrimental beliefs many times and the outcomes were great.

Now, here's the exercise that will allow you to easily and effectively change any behavior. I have found similar exercises in the book NLP Patterns for Success Mastery, authored by Charles Faulkner and Roberta McDonald. I've modified it, adding some elements and changing the others. I hold that this exercise is far more effective in this new form.

Begin with reading all the steps and my notes. Start with the exercise once you're finished reading.

1. Think about the belief that you want to change.
2. What negative consequences does this belief bring into your life? Write them down.
3. Specify the new belief (opposite of the old one), give it a positive form, e.g. use *"I'm open to new relationships,"* instead of, *"I'm not closed to new relationships."*
4. What positive consequences will faith in this new belief bring you? How will you feel? How will you behave? What will change? Give yourself a moment to deeply reflect on these questions.
5. Ask yourself, *"What would a person with this belief do?"* Imagine various behaviors and actions. Write down three or four behaviors of this kind.
6. Pick one behavior/action from the ones you have wrote down, that will serve you as the first proof of the new belief. Consider when this kind of situation can happen in your life and choose an exact date and place. The moment you choose will be the moment when the new belief will appear.
7. See yourself in the future, in the place and time you have picked, acting as you have described it. From the observer's point of view, imagine how the "future you" does that can be a proof of your future desired belief. Make it a short movie with yourself starring in a main role and watch it until the end.
8. Rewind the scene to the beginning. Now get into it, see what happens from the perspective of your own eyes. Play this future scene as if it was happening now. Use

all of your senses to feel what's happening. At the end, hear yourself confidently speaking out loud your new belief. Watch until it ends.

9. Repeat steps 7 to 8 three times, choosing a different action and a different time and place every single time.

Notes: Write down all consequences and actions on a sheet of paper. It's very important as writing these down makes you realize important relationships between them. The realization alone can have a huge impact on you. When it comes to action, they have to be the ones that can really happen in your life. The best choice is to pick actions that can happen in the timespan of the nearest month. If you want to believe you can easily start conversations with other people, the actions could be the following: 1. You approach three different strangers and start talking with them on whatever topic; 2. You spot your old friends somewhere on the streets and start fun conversation with them; 3. You talk with your parents/family, discussing even the strangest topic.

Before a belief can come into an existence, it has to be proven real. This exercise makes you see these proofs in your head. The new belief is now installed, but not as firmly as you'd want it to. So, as soon as you get an occasion to do these things in the real world—**take action and do them immediately**! Once your mind gets real proof in form of a concrete action that goes well with your belief, the belief will get rooted in your belief system very firmly.

Chapter 22: A Few Words about Meditation

Meditation is of the greatest habits you can acquire to develop your emotional intelligence and wisdom. The best benefit comes from a new way of experiencing moments in your life, no matter whether they are unique or completely normal.

Even if you're just having your everyday evening walk around the park in your neighborhood, you can deeply experience what's happening around you when you are living "here and now." You can feel real calmness, peace and pleasure coming from being present in the moment. It also applies to your entire life, every single moment of which it consists. When you are present in the moment, there is no stress, there are no thoughts, no worries—just peace. No matter if you are driving a car, partying, looking into your lover's eyes or simply staring at the wall in your room—once you become aware of the moment, you will want to return to this state really often.

There are many more benefits to entering this state of awareness. Once your mind processes are turned off, **your mind gets clear and keen-edged like a laser-sharpened razor. Your senses sharpen up and your attention increases.** This is the key to efficiency in all life areas (in sports, for example). In the here and now, you are capable of much, much more.

It's also one of the best ways to improve your communication and social skills. You will see that once you stop constantly thinking about what to say and how to lead the conversation, it flows nicely, not encountering any obstacles. You just say what your consciousness gives you and it turns out they are always the best things you could have said in that moment. Moreover, you will become alert and you will be able to see much more in other people's body language and communication—many subtle changes in the tone of voice, and verbal language being used.

Any time you experience great moments, thanks to meditation you are finally able to experience them fully. It's as if someone took off a heavy curtain covering your head. This curtain consists of thought processes that usually cover the true nature of things, judging, criticizing and blindfolding you.

The so-called "up-time" is a skill that can be learned and attained. The more you practice, the easier it will get to enter that state and remaining there for a long time. I'm now able to get into the "now" almost anytime I want, without any warm-ups, just when I want it. It's as natural as raising my arm or moving my leg. I just practiced a lot and you can get there too.

In the beginning, it is good to support yourself using some exercises that will help you enter that state.

Here's one I want to share with you in this book.

The point of this exercise is to overload your mind with stimuli. After such overload, your mind will switch off for a moment and you will get into strong "stand up-time".

It's also a great warm-up for your mind.

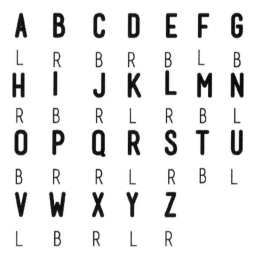

On the drawing above you can see two lines of letters. The bigger ones are, obviously, the alphabet letters, which you have to read aloud during this exercise. The smaller letters under the alphabet—L, R and B—show you which arm to rise when you're reading each letter of the alphabet. L stands for Left, R for Right, and B for Both arms.

So, the exercise boils down to you reading the alphabet and raising your arms up according to the small letters.

It's easier to do it standing up. Try being as fast as possible, and once you reach the end, start over. Go through four loops, then another four, this time reading the alphabet from the end to the beginning. If you make a mistake, don't correct yourself, just continue! After you're done (that should take a few minutes), turn your look away from the screen and start observing the world around you.

You mind backed off. You are now in the present moment!

You can do this exercise as often as you want. After some time, you will get used to this drawing and it won't be able to make your mind confused and tired anymore. You can then come up with your own, even more difficult picture, with the letters of the alphabet out of order. Then, you can ask someone to ask you some abstract and stupid questions when you're doing this exercise, to make the task even harder.

Since this book's subject is emotional intelligence, not meditation, I just wanted to show you what can be done and what the benefits are. If you want to learn more about meditation (and I think you really should, the list of profits is almost endless), I also wrote another book, which hit the Amazon bestsellers list a few times, exclusively on the fascinating topic of meditation. Here it is: http://tinyurl.com/ianmeditationkindle

It will provide you with all the info you need to start your soothing and enlightening journey with meditation.

BONUS CHAPTER: VISUALIZATIONS 101

Since this book tells you to use visualization very often, and that's something some people have slight trouble with, I decided to add this chapter to help you better see your mental images. Again, it contains three practical and very effective exercises that will help you visualize better and with bigger intensity, or take your visualization techniques to the next level. Visualization is a key to many tools, not only connected with NLP, but also with effective learning, goal setting, maintaining motivation and positive thinking, so it's really worth it to establish this skill on a decent level!

Self-development can be defined as a pursuit of the desired condition. Since the state you want to achieve lies somewhere in the future, your ability to see what you actually want to achieve is one of very crucial parts of the bigger picture.

Without a preview on how our lives should look like in the future, it's much more difficult to make real changes in the present. That's why rich and colorful visualizations that can totally devour you are so important. When you add sounds, smells, flavors and inner feelings, the references created in your brain can be so strong your subconscious will automatically focus all its attention on achieving your goal and will maintain that state for a long time.

No matter if you have trouble with seeing the internal images at all, or they get distorted and unclear, regular use of these exercises will enable you to create sharp, clear and detail-saturated visualizations.

Exercise I

- Go to a silent place, preferably your room, with doors closed. Close your eyes and recall any situation from your life, preferably a nice memory. Don't try to see the images at this point, but focus on hearing sounds which accompanied that memory. Take a moment to listen to what happened there. What sounds are there?

Is anybody saying anything? What's the manner, tempo and volume of their speech? Hear what you heard then.

- Now, add a sense of touch to this. In your imagination, touch something that was there, any object, piece of clothing, whatever. Feel the surface of this object, its texture, temperature, weight. Get into that memory...
- Now, add all the scents that were there. Feel the smell of the air... and then...
- What do you see? See the images that appear. Maintain it and enjoy the view. You've just fully created your visualization.

This exercise is about activating any other senses than sight at first, which makes it much easier to bring back the image associated with that memory. It happens because every piece of information is saved in different parts of the brain. **Not only does the information about memories contain visual data**, but also auditory, sensory, etc., so that the increased activity in other parts of the brain helps you activate the sense of vision in your imagination and put it all together.

Exercise II

- Choose any object from your room. It can be a phone, computer screen, book or anything else. Put that object somewhere close to you, so you can look at it freely. Observe it thoroughly for about five seconds.
- After that, close your eyes and visualize exactly what you have just seen. Keep the image of this object as long as you can. If the image goes away, it doesn't matter. Open your eyes and start again.
- After a few series, choose another object and repeat the same process—observe it for five seconds, then close your eyes and visualize it thoroughly.
- Do this exercise five minutes a day, every day.

Practiced regularly, this exercise will give you the ability to create clear and accurate images on demand. It's just a matter of training—you will see that day after day the visualizations will be becoming increasingly natural for you.

Once you master bringing back the images of objects you normally see around you, modify it and create imaginary things in your mind.

Create abstractions of various kinds and keep them in your imagination as long as possible.

Exercise III

- Open a book, preferably a fiction story you like. Randomly pick a page and start reading.
- After a few lines, stop reading and close your eyes.
- Start imagining all this you have just read about. Try to notice as many details as possible: people who are there, environment in which they are, the words they speak.
- Create this visualization for a minute, then go back to reading.
- After another few lines, close your eyes and start creating inner images again. Repeat this for about five minutes.
- Practice daily.

Literature is often rich in colorful, detailed descriptions that often help improve imagination. The fact of reading about what's in the picture often automatically creates the picture itself. In this exercise, you will additionally be able to consciously focus on that visualization, seeing many more details.

You can use the exercises above together, or you could also pick one or two of them, the ones that suit you the most. **Remember to practice regularly.** It's like riding a bicycle —once you learn it, you will always be able to do it, as it will become perfectly natural to you. The ability to get into rich visualizations is a key that opens many self-development doors. You will finally be able to visualize a successful future, get rid of bad memories using NLP, remember difficult things using memorization techniques, and do many other useful things. Good luck!

Conclusion

Thank you again for choosing this book. You've just made the first step in this great and long journey of emotional intelligence mastery. Knowing that this is one of the most important skills you can possibly possess in this life, now all you have to do is to **TAKE ACTION**. Go back to all these exercises, practice and never give up. It is always difficult to start something new, but usually the beginning turns out to be the most difficult part. After you gain your momentum, see the proof in real results and acquire new beliefs, it will be a no-brainer type of deal. You will just keep going, knowing you are on the right path. The path to a happy and successful life. Remember, most people don't even want to change at all. The fact that you've decided to do something with your life really means a lot!

One last thing before you go – Can I ask you a favor? I need your help! If you like this book, could you please share your experience on Amazon and write an honest review? It will be just one minute for you (I will be happy even with one sentence!), but a GREAT help for me :)

Here's link: http://tinyurl.com/reviewmyeqbook

Since I'm not a well-established author and I don't have powerful people and big publishing companies supporting me, I read every single review and jump around with joy like a little kid every time my readers comment on one of my books and give me their honest feedback! If I was able to inspire you in any way, please let me know! It will also help me get my books in front of more people looking for new ideas and useful knowledge. If you did not enjoy the book or had a problem with it, please don't hesitate to contact me at contact@mindfulnessforsuccess.com and tell me how I can improve it to provide more value and more knowledge to my readers. I'm constantly working on my books to make them better and more helpful.

Thank you and good luck! I believe in you and I wish you all the best on your new journey! Your friend,

Ian

My Free Gift to You
Discover How to Get Rid of Stress & Anxiety and Reach Inner Peace in 20
Days or Less!

To help speed up your personal transformation, I have prepared a special gift for you!
Download my full, 120 page e-book "Mindfulness Based Stress and Anxiety
Management Tools" (Value: $9.99) for free.

Moreover, by becoming my subscriber, you will be the first one to **get my new books**
for only $0.99, during their short two day promotional launch. **I passionately write**
about: social dynamics, career, Neuro-Linguistic Programming, goal achieving, positive
psychology and philosophy, life hacking, meditation and becoming the most awesome
version of yourself. Additionally, once a week I will send you insightful tips and **free e-**
book offers to keep you on track on your journey to becoming the best you!

That's my way of saying **"thank you"** to my new and established readers and helping you
grow. I hate spam and e-mails that come too frequently – **you will never receive more**
than one email a week! Guaranteed.

Just follow this link:
tinyurl.com/mindfulnessgift

Hey there like-minded friends, let's get connected!

Don't hesitate to visit:

-My blog: www.mindfulnessforsuccess.com

-My facebook fanpage: https://www.facebook.com/mindfulnessforsuccess

-My twitter: https://twitter.com/mindfulness78

Twitter handle: @Mindfulness4Success

My Instagram profile: https://instagram.com/mindfulnessforsuccess

I hope to see you there!

Recommended Reading for You

If you are interested in Self-Development, NLP, Psychology, Social Dynamics, PR, Soft Skills and related topics, you might be interested in previewing or downloading my other books:

Communication Skills Training: A Practical Guide to Improving Your Social Intelligence, Presentation, Persuasion and Public Speaking

Do You Know How To Communicate With People Effectively, Avoid Conflicts and Get What You Want From Life?

...It's not only about what you say, but also about WHEN, WHY and HOW you say it.

Do The Things You Usually Say Help You, Or Maybe Hold You Back?

Have you ever considered **how many times you intuitively felt that maybe you lost something important or crucial, simply because you unwittingly said or did something, which put somebody off?** Maybe it was a misfortunate word, bad formulation, inappropriate joke, forgotten name, huge misinterpretation, awkward conversation or a strange tone of your voice?
Maybe you assumed that you knew exactly what a particular concept meant for another person and you stopped asking questions?
Maybe you could not listen carefully or could not stay silent for a moment? **How many times have you wanted to achieve something, negotiate better terms, or ask for a promotion and failed miserably?**

It's time to put that to an end with the help of this book.

<u>Lack of communication skills is exactly what ruins most peoples' lives.</u>
If you don't know how to communicate properly, you are going to have problems both in your intimate and family relationships.

You are going to be ineffective in work and business situations. It's going to be troublesome managing employees or getting what you want from your boss or your clients on a daily basis. Overall, **effective communication is like an engine oil which makes your life run**

smoothly, getting you wherever you want to be. There are very few areas in life in which you can succeed in the long run without this crucial skill.

What Will You Learn With This Book?

-What Are The **Most Common Communication Obstacles** Between People And How To Avoid Them
-How To Express Anger And Avoid Conflicts
-What Are **The Most 8 Important Questions You Should Ask Yourself** If You Want To Be An Effective Communicator?
-**5 Most Basic and Crucial** Conversational Fixes
-How To Deal With Difficult and Toxic People
-Phrases to **Purge from Your Dictionary** (And What to Substitute Them With)
-The Subtle Art of **Giving and Receiving Feedback**
-Rapport, the **Art of Excellent Communication**
-How to Use Metaphors to **Communicate Better** And **Connect With People**
-What Metaprograms and Meta Models Are and How Exactly To Make Use of Them To **Become A Polished Communicator**
-How To Read Faces and **How to Effectively Predict Future Behaviors**
-How to Finally Start **Remembering Names**
-How to Have a Great Public Presentation
-How To Create Your Own **Unique Personality** in Business (and Everyday Life)
-Effective Networking

Direct link to Amazon Kindle Store: https://tinyurl.com/IanCommSkillsKindle

Paperback version on Createspace:

http://tinyurl.com/iancommunicationpaperback

Natural Confidence Training: How to Develop Healthy Self-Esteem and Deep Self-Confidence to Be Successful and Become True Friends with Yourself

Lack of self-confidence and problems with unhealthy self-esteem are usually the reason why smart, competent and talented people never achieve a satisfying life, a life that should easily be possible for them.

Think about your childhood.
At the age of four or five, there weren't too many things that you considered impossible, right?
You weren't bothered or held back by any kind of criticism; you stayed indifferent to what other people thought of you. An ugly stain on your sweater, or even worse, on your leggings, was not considered a problem or an obstacle.

You could run on a crowded beach absolutely nude, laughing, go swimming in a city fountain and then play in the sandbox with strawberry ice cream smeared in your hair. Nothing and no one could stop you from saying what you wanted to say, even the silliest things. **There was no shame in your early childhood;** you loved yourself and everyone else.

Can you remember it?
What happened to us?

Parents, teachers, preachers and media **stuffed certain beliefs into your head**, day after day for many years. These beliefs and attitudes **robbed you of your natural, inborn confidence.**
Maybe it was one traumatic experience of some kind that changed you, or maybe it was a slow process that lasted for years. One thing is certain—lacking confidence is not your natural, default state. **It brings you down and now you have to unlearn it.**

Can you name even a single situation in life where high confidence isn't useful?
... Right?

Confidence is not useful only in everyday life and casual situations. Do you really want to fulfill your dreams, or do you just want to keep chatting about them with your friends, until one day you wake up as a grumpy, old, frustrated person?

Big achievements require brave and fearless actions. If you want to act bravely,

you need to be confident.
Along with lots of useful, practical exercises, this book will provide you with plenty of new information that will help you understand what confidence problems really come down to. And this is the most important and the saddest part, because most people do not truly recognize the root problem, and that's why they get poor results.

In this book you will read about:
-How, when and why society robs us all of natural confidence and healthy self-esteem.
-What kind of social and psychological traps you need to avoid to feel much calmer, happier and more confident.
-What "natural confidence" means and how it becomes natural.
-What "self-confidence" really is and what it definitely isn't (as opposed to what most people think!).
-How your mind hurts you when it really just wants to help you, and how to stop the process.
-What different kinds of fear we feel, where they come from and how to defeat them.
-How to have a great relationship with yourself.
-What beliefs and habits you should have and cultivate to succeed.
-How to use stress to boost your inner strength.
-Effective and ineffective ways of building healthy self-esteem.
-How mindfulness and meditation help boost, cultivate and maintain your natural confidence.
-Why the relation between self-acceptance and stress is so crucial.
-How to stay confident in professional situations.
-How to protect your self-esteem when life brings you down and how to deal with criticism and jealousy.
-How to use neuro-linguistic programming, imagination, visualizations, diary entries and your five senses to re-program your subconscious and get rid of "mental viruses" and detrimental beliefs that actively destroy your natural confidence and healthy self-esteem.

In the last part of the book you will find 15 of the most effective, proven and field-tested strategies and exercises that help people transform their lives.

Take the right action and start changing your life for the better today!

Direct Buy Link to Amazon Kindle Store:

https://tinyurl.com/IanConfidenceTraining

https://tinyurl.com/IanConfidencePaperback

Meditation for Beginners: How to Meditate (as an Ordinary Person!) to Relieve Stress and Be Successful

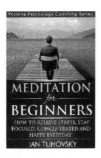

Meditation doesn't have to be about crystals, hypnotic folk music and incense sticks! **Forget about sitting in unnatural and uncomfortable positions while going, "Ommmmm...."** It is not necessarily a club full of yoga masters, Shaolin monks, hippies and new-agers.

It is a super useful and universal practice which can improve your overall brain performance and happiness. When meditating, you take a step back from actively thinking your thoughts, and instead see them for what they are. The reason why meditation is helpful in reducing stress and attaining peace is that it gives your over-active consciousness a break.

Just like your body needs it, your mind does too!

I give you the gift of peace that I was able to attain through present moment awareness.

Direct Buy Link to Amazon Kindle Store: https://tinyurl.com/IanMeditationGuide
Paperback version on Createspace: http://tinyurl.com/ianmeditationpaperback

Zen: Beginner's Guide: Happy, Peaceful and Focused Lifestyle for Everyone

Contrary to popular belief, Zen is not a discipline reserved for monks practicing Kung Fu. Although there is some truth to this idea, Zen is a practice that is applicable, useful and pragmatic for anyone to study regardless of what religion you follow (or don't follow).

Zen is the practice of studying your subconscious and **seeing your true nature.** The purpose of this work is to show you how to apply and utilize the teachings and essence of Zen in everyday life in the Western society. I'm not really an "absolute truth seeker" unworldly type of person—I just believe in practical plans and blueprints that actually help in living a better life. Of course I will tell you about the origin of Zen and the traditional ways of practicing it, but I will also show you my side of things, my personal point of view and translation of many Zen truths into a more "contemporary" and practical language.
It is a "modern Zen lifestyle" type of book.

What You Will Read About:
• Where Did Zen Come from? - A short history and explanation of Zen
• What Does Zen Teach? - The major teachings and precepts of Zen
• Various Zen meditation techniques that are applicable and practical for everyone!
• The Benefits of a Zen Lifestyle
• What Zen Buddhism is NOT?
• How to Slow Down and Start Enjoying Your Life
• How to Accept Everything and Lose Nothing
• Why Being Alone Can Be Beneficial
• Why Pleasure Is NOT Happiness
• Six Ways to Practically Let Go
• How to De-clutter Your Life and Live Simply
• "Mindfulness on Steroids"
• How to Take Care of Your Awareness and Focus
• Where to Start and How to Practice Zen as a Regular Person
• And many other interesting concepts...

I invite you to take this journey into the peaceful world of Zen Buddhism with me today!

Direct Buy Link to Amazon Kindle Store: https://tinyurl.com/IanZenGuide
Paperback version on Createspace: http://tinyurl.com/ianzenpaperback

Buddhism: Beginner's Guide: Bring Peace and Happiness to Your Everyday Life

Buddhism is one of the most practical and simple belief systems on this planet, and it has greatly helped me on my way to become a better person in every aspect possible. In this book I will show you what happened and how it was.

No matter if you are totally green when it comes to Buddha's teachings or maybe you have already heard something about them—this book will help you systematize your knowledge and will inspire you to learn more and to take steps to make your life positively better!

I invite you to take this beautiful journey into the graceful and meaningful world of Buddhism with me today!

Direct Buy Link to Amazon Kindle Store: https://tinyurl.com/IanBuddhismGuide
Paperback version on Createspace: http://tinyurl.com/ianbuddhismpaperback

Speed Reading: How to Read 3-5 Times Faster and Become an Effective Learner

No matter if your objective is to **do great during your university exams**, become a **bestselling writer** or start **your own business,** you will have to read A LOT, and I mean it. Reading takes time. **Time is our most valuable asset**—nothing new here. You can always make money or meet new friends, but **you will never be able to "make time."** The only way to succeed and have a happy life without regrets is to use it wisely and **learn how to manage and save it.**

In this book, I will take you through the dynamics of speed reading in a way you may have never imagined before. I'm here to preach the need for speed reading and make use of some of the principles that can steer your knowledge and productivity in the right direction.

Learn How to Read 5 Times Faster, Remember Much More and Save Massive Time!

In This Book You Will Read About:
• The History of Speed Reading
• Popular Speed Reading Myths
• **Environment and Preparation**
• How to Measure Your Reading Speed
• **Key Speed Reading Techniques**
• Reading Tips for Computer and Tablet

- Common Reading Mistakes to Avoid
- Easy and Effective Memory/Learning Techniques
- **Dealing with Tests and Diagrams**
- **Practical Exercises and Eye Adjustments**
- Useful Links and Ideas
- Diet
- How to Track Your Progress
- Proper Motivation and Mindset

Direct Buy Link to Amazon Kindle Store: https://tinyurl.com/IanSpeedReading

Paperback version on Createspace: http://tinyurl.com/ianreadingpaperback

About The Author

Author's blog: www.mindfulnessforsuccess.com
Amazon Author Page: amazon.com/author/iantuhovsky

Hi! I'm Ian...

. . . and I am interested in life. I'm in the study of having an awesome and passionate life, which I believe is within the reach of practically everyone. I'm not a mentor or a guru. I'm just a guy who always knew there was more than we are told. I managed to turn my life around from way below my expectations to a really satisfying life, and now I want to share this fascinating journey with you so that you can do it, too.

I was born and raised somewhere in Eastern Europe, where Polar Bears eat people on the streets, we munch on snow instead of ice-cream and there's only vodka instead of tap water, but since I make a living out of several different businesses, I move to a new country every couple of months. I also work as an HR consultant for various European companies.

I love self-development, traveling, recording music and providing value by helping others. I passionately read and write about social psychology, sociology, NLP, meditation, mindfulness, eastern philosophy, emotional intelligence, time management, communication skills and all of the topics related to conscious self-development and being the most awesome version of yourself.

Breathe. Relax. Feel that you're alive and smile. And never hesitate to contact me!